Mexican Americans & Health

MEXICAN AMERICAN STUDIES SERIES

Adela de la Torre
EDITOR

Mexican Americans & Health

¡SANA! ¡SANA!

Adela de la Torre
& Antonio L. Estrada

The University of Arizona Press   Tucson

First Printing
The University of Arizona Press
© 2001 The Arizona Board of Regents

⊛ This book is printed on acid-free, archival-quality paper.
Manufactured in the United States of America

06   05   04   03   02   01   6   5   4   3   2   1

Library of Congress Cataloging-in-Publication Data
Torre, Adela de la.
Mexican Americans and health : ¡sana! ¡sana! / Adela de la Torre and Antonio L.
Estrada.
      p. cm. — (Mexican American studies series)
Includes bibliographical references and index.
    ISBN 0-8165-1976-5
    1. Mexican Americans—Health and hygiene. 2. Mexican Americans—Medical
care. 3. Minorities—Health and hygiene. 4. Minorities—Medical care. I. Estrada,
Antonio L. II. Title. III. Series.
RA448.5.M4 T67 2001
362.1′089′6872073—dc21
00-012932

British Library Cataloguing-in-Publication Data
A catalogue record for this book is available from the British Library.

Sana, sana,
Colita de rana.
Si no sanas hoy,
Sanarás mañana.

> *Get well, get well,*
> *Little frog tail.*
> *If today you don't get well,*
> *Tomorrow you will be well.*

■ Traditional saying recited to comfort a child while rubbing the site of a pain or injury

To my family, my daughters Adelita and Gaby, my mother Herminia Domitila, my Tía Tanna, my husband Stephen, and the memory of my beloved Abuelita Adela. Their constant support and encouragement make all things possible.

—Adela de la Torre

To my wife Barbara, my children Charlene and Gloria, my father Antonio, and all my family who have provided me with endless support and encouragement over the years.

—Antonio L. Estrada

■ CONTENTS

■ FIGURES

■ TABLES

■ ACRONYMS USED IN THE TEXT

AAMC	American Association of Medical Colleges
AFDC	Aid to Families with Dependent Children
AHCCCS	Arizona Health Care Cost Containment System, the Arizona equivalent of Medicaid
AIDS	acquired immunodeficiency syndrome
CDC	Centers for Disease Control and Prevention
DAWN	Drug Abuse Warning Network
DTP	diphtheria-tetanus-pertussis vaccine
HHANES	Hispanic Health and Nutrition Examination Survey
HIV	human immunodeficiency virus
HPV	human papillomavirus
HRSA	U.S. Health Resources and Services Administration
IDU	injection drug user
INS	Immigration and Naturalization Service
IRCA	Immigration Reform and Control Act
NHANES III	Third National Health and Nutrition Examination Survey
NIDA	National Institute on Drug Abuse
NIDDM	non-insulin-dependent diabetes mellitus
NIH	National Institutes of Health
PCP	phenyl cyclohexyl piperidine, or angel dust
SAMHSA	Substance Abuse and Mental Health Services Administration
SSA	Social Security Administration
SSI	Supplemental Security Income
STD	sexually transmitted disease

ACKNOWLEDGMENTS

This book would not have been possible without the help of several people. We would like to take this opportunity to acknowledge their efforts and thank them for their assistance and participation in this project. First, we would like to thank the undergraduate students at the University of Arizona who conducted the community interviews that are an integral part of this book. They include Carlos R. Acuña, Maria Acuña, Susan Ammouri, Maria G. Broadway, Malala Elston, Brooke E. Felker, Marco A. Gámez, Rori Kelly, Daniel B. Lobato, Norma G. Navarro, Cynthia Nevarez, Olivia Nuñez, Olivia Palacios, Belinda Rodriguez, and Joseph Urbina, Jr.

We would also like to extend our thanks to graduate students Erynn Masi de Casanova and Maritza De La Trinidad for their patience and the significant contributions they made through their excellent research, writing, editing, and coordinating skills. In addition, we would like to express our gratitude to Thomas Gelsinon and Kirsteen E. Anderson for giving us the benefit of their editorial expertise. We would also like to thank cartographers Gary Christopherson and Carol Placchi for developing the original maps for the text (figures 1 through 6). Finally, we would like to acknowledge Patti Hartmann for her vision and support for this project.

"I'm healthy but . . ."

INTRODUCTION

Mexican Americans and Health is the inaugural volume in the Mexican American Studies series. Since this book is intended primarily as an undergraduate textbook, we have tried to make it as accessible as possible. At the end of each chapter, readers will find a set of discussion questions that serve as a review of key content in the chapter. In addition to source notes and a bibliography listing print and Internet sources we relied on, we provide a list of suggested readings for anyone wishing to study a topic in more depth. Technical and Spanish-language terms are defined in a glossary at the end of the book. Words that appear in the glossary are in boldface on first reference in every chapter as a signal to turn to the glossary for more detailed explanation of that term.

The rapid growth of the Mexican American population and the increasing interest in issues of human diversity has created a need for introductory texts that address critical issues in the Mexican American community. We hope this book will provide insight into a long-neglected issue: namely, the cultural, linguistic, and financial factors that influence how Mexican Americans access—or fail to access—the U.S. health care system.

 ## Overview of Health Care Issues for People of Mexican Origin

Many factors influence the health of the Mexican-origin population of the United States. For example, individual health is intricately related to social and population conditions as well as genetic factors. Although this group shares certain **health status** and access issues with other minorities—African Americans, Native Americans, and Asian Americans—some issues affect people of Mexican descent in distinct ways. Although historical and political-geographic factors affect the overall health status of **Mexican Americans,** the literature on Mexican American health often ignores these factors. Yet, historical context is how this group defines its identity and its social location within the broader U.S. society. This, in turn, influences how its members enter the health care system and how they are treated within it.

Elaborating on the issue of identity and social location requires that we understand the deep roots Mexican Americans have in the U.S. Southwest, which for centuries was Mexican territory. These roots predate the incorporation of this region into the United States. Moreover, discrimination, which has influenced the **educational attainment** and **occupational location** of Mexican Americans, is linked to their historical and political incorporation, or lack thereof, within the U.S. Southwest.

With this in mind, we selected the term *Mexican-origin population* to include people who are Mexican **immigrants** as well as **native-born** Mexican Americans. Although other terms such as **Chicano/Chicana** and **Latino/Latina** are often used, they are less specific to the Mexican-origin population based on self-report U.S. census data. The term **Hispanic** is a broader category including other subgroups such as Puerto Ricans, Cubans, Central Americans, and other census-designated Hispanic subgroups. Where possible, we attempt to use data specific to people of Mexican origin. However, these data are available only for certain health status categories, so we have had to use data from the overall Hispanic population for some health indicators.

Throughout this text, we also integrate voices of Mexican-origin people to illustrate how their experiences frame health issues. For example, in chapter 1 we will show how family location decisions contribute to the concentration of Mexican Americans in the Southwest. This is clearly explained by our interviewees Carmen and Marco:

> Actually . . . I didn't have a choice directly as the decision had been made generations before me as to where the family would set root and they did so because the Santa Cruz Valley at that time was very fertile and very green. The river was flowing and the climate was pleasant; it was just an ideal location. (Carmen G., 49)

> I finally met up with my mother and with my brother . . . two or three years after he [my brother] went to San Diego. [I came to the Southwest] because my family was here. I don't know why they chose the Southwest, probably because of proximity [to Mexico]. (Marco G., 28)

The voices of everyday people such as Carmen and Marco will help demonstrate how the Mexican-origin population experiences health and health care, and how their experience is linked to their cultural roots. It is just as important to listen to these voices in the twenty-first century as it was in the twentieth. The voices of the *abuelas, tíos, padres, hermanas,* and *hijos* (grandparents, aunts and uncles, parents, sisters, and children) to whom you will be introduced offer guidance in the development of health care strategies that will result in better health for Mexican Americans and the nation as a whole.

We have developed a model that serves as an underlying framework in understanding the most influential factors that affect the health status of Mexican Americans and the way the health care system responds to this group. The following flow chart illustrates how different components influence the health status of the U.S. Mexican-origin population.

Starting from the left of the diagram, we see how the historical experiences and political-geographic location of the Mexican-origin population influence sociodemographic (social and population) factors such as occupation and immigrant status. These sociodemographic **variables** influence **health care access** (financial) issues, environmental and behavioral health issues, and cultural factors, which in turn influence the health status of this group. Genetic factors also play a role in health status, as they do for everyone, but they are not directly influenced by these other factors. An overarching structural element that affects the health status of this group, and other groups, is the U.S. health care delivery system. Ultimately, this system provides both opportunities and barriers to the Mexican-origin population. Although constructed independently of the Mexican American community, this system has a profound influence on the group's future social, economic, and health well-being.

The chapter numbers on the diagram indicate where we will discuss each of these important factors. By the end of the book, we hope that readers will have a broader understanding of the complex issues surrounding the health and health care of the U.S. Mexican-origin population. The following is a brief overview of each of the chapters.

In chapter 1 we discuss the historical roots and political-geographic concentration of Mexican-origin people in the Southwest and elsewhere. These factors have fostered cultural resiliency and affect the group's perceptions of health care and disease, as well as how they view the dominant society. This chapter also examines socioeconomic status, which is often the

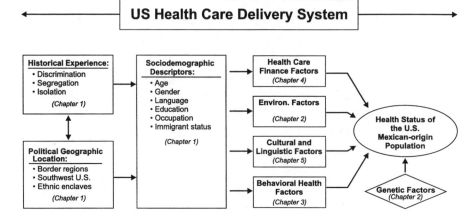

Factors Influencing the Health Status of Mexican Americans

main predictor of health status and health care access. For example, one reason Mexican Americans fare more poorly than the dominant society in terms of jobs and education is that the current demand for cheap labor in the industrial and agricultural sectors of the economy requires the constant flow of immigrant labor, primarily from Mexico. Gracie's childhood memories clearly illustrate this point:

> Being poor, my father never gave it a second thought about taking me to the emergency room. Instead he told my mother to take me to the hospital in the morning. . . . So my mother woke me up. At that time I think I was so exhausted from vomiting and the pain was so strong that I was kicking and I nearly kicked a hole in the wall. . . . Mind you my mother didn't know English so I had to translate for her. So I was coming in and out of consciousness and finally we made it to the hospital, a public hospital in Houston. . . . My mother was holding me in her arms, and if it had not been for the fact that the doctor just happened to be going through the lobby area, and saw me pass out, and noticed the purple lips, I would probably be dead. . . . He realized that my appendix had burst at that moment and quickly rushed me to the emergency room for immediate surgery. (Gracie S., 46)

Much of the recent literature that focuses on health and health care access examines variables such as educational attainment, poverty status, occupational location, and marital status, as these data explain much of the difference in health status between the Mexican-origin population and other groups. Cultural variables, such as immigrant status and mastery of English, are other strong influences that affect how well individual people of Mexican origin are integrated into the health care system. Language status, language choice, and linguistic discrimination influence level of education and, ultimately, economic status, which in turn influences health status. Another important factor that differentiates this Hispanic **subpopulation** is the perceived origin of the discrimination experienced by this group. Unlike other Hispanic subpopulations, such as Cuban Americans and Central Americans, the experience of racial and ethnic discrimination for Mexicans is rooted in the historical conquest of the Southwest and the loss of homeland, language, and culture. Making matters worse are the economic dependency of Mexico on the U.S. economy and American dependence on low-wage Mexican labor in agriculture and other industries. These factors have created an underclass of immigrants and increased racial tensions and divisions in the Southwest and elsewhere. Thus, it is not surprising to find **racialized** labor markets where the concentration of Mexican immigrants is high. In low-wage sectors, working conditions are often terrible and employee health insurance is not provided, which ultimately has a big effect on the health status of workers. These low-wage sectors include the farm labor market, the non-unionized service sector, and the manufacturing sector. Marco, reflecting on his experiences as a worker in the service sector, states:

> As far as the pay is concerned and the load of work they have to do, it is bullshit. . . . they are worked to death. . . . Some of these ladies are going well into their fifties, and they are doing manual labor. I mean it is heavy work. There are times when I leave work, after I've worked a dinner function, and I will walk back to the dishwashing room and it's hot and they have hundreds of dishes and it's two people. . . . they're understaffed and they are underpaid. (Marco G., 28)

Chapter 2 presents the health status of the Mexican-origin population relative to the rest of the population. Despite the low socioeconomic status of many Mexican Americans, there is an interesting phenomenon known as the Mexican American **morbidity** and **mortality** paradox. Even though Mexican-origin individuals have a low socioeconomic status, similar to that of African Americans, morbidity (illness) and mortality (death) data do not reflect the same effects of economic and social disadvantage as for African Americans. This concept has been applied most frequently to childbearing women. If we look at infant mortality rates for low-income Mexican immigrants, we find very good birth outcomes, which is not the case for African Americans. Nonetheless, there are health problems that pose concerns for the Mexican-origin community. For children, these include childhood **obesity**, lack of immunizations, and oral health problems. The problem of oral health affects young adults also, as explained by Lily, a twenty-year-old college student:

> I'm healthy, but I know that when it comes to going to the dentist I need to see somebody. And, I know that it's expensive to go. I was in the doctor's office and he said you need to get your wisdom teeth out, but it costs a lot of money and I can't. . . . I even went to talk to someone to see if I could apply for **Medicaid**. . . . just to have backup while at the university. (Lily Q., 20)

The most significant health problems for women are related to prenatal care, preventable cancers such as cervical cancer, and domestic violence. For Mexican-origin workers who have jobs in agriculture, occupational hazards include work-related injuries, pesticide poisoning, heat-related conditions, musculoskeletal disorders, and communicable diseases. Major health problems of the adult population include diabetes, cardiovascular disease (heart disease and heart attack), cancer (in particular colorectal and lung cancer), substance abuse, and HIV/AIDS. In light of these health issues, it is important to develop culturally sensitive, community-based health care for the Mexican-origin population. To do so, we must consider the cultural values of this population in our health care interventions. Values such as **machismo, familismo**, and **marianismo** influence care-seeking decisions and treatment of illness.

Chapter 3 discusses the behavioral health issues affecting Mexican Americans. Substance abuse, HIV and AIDS, and violence are major problems, but there are little data specific to this group. To date the data indicate that these problems may develop differently in people of Mexican origin than in other Latino/a subpopulations. For example, drug abuse seems to have an early onset in Mexican-origin youth. The peer norms of this group are also somewhat favorable to drug dealing as a source of income, given the limited economic opportunities for Mexican-origin youth as well as their concentration in low-income **ethnic enclaves**.

Acculturation and demographic (population) factors influence the type of drug used and the frequency of use by children and adults. There is conflicting evidence concerning the role of Mexican American cultural identity in drug use. Depending on individual circumstances, it may be risk reducing or risk enhancing. For example, someone who strongly identifies with Mexican American culture may not use drugs because Mexican values and behavior do not support drug use. However, these values and behaviors conflict with the dominant culture. Thus, the additional stress to conform to the dominant culture while maintaining a strong cultural identity may increase the risk of drug use. This dilemma is exemplified by the identity struggle experienced by Marco in his youth:

> When I first arrived, I remember getting beat up and I remember fighting because the kids called me "wetback," "greaser," you name it. I remember going to the principal's office twice a week [because of] a fight. It got to the point where I couldn't attend school anymore. The same situation happened to my brother, but then it stopped. I asked him, "How come no one is beating you up anymore?" He said that one of his teachers had recommended that he tell kids that he was from Spain. Sure enough, I went to school [and said] I was from Spain and I never got busted. It was the coolest thing that anyone had ever heard of . . . so for a long time I was telling kids that I was from Spain and they thought I was pretty cool. But, you know, deep inside I am a Mexican, I am a Chicano, and that was taken away from me. (Marco G., 28)

Other significant factors related to substance abuse include socioeconomic status, peer pressure, and family influence. Confounding these variables is the role of drugs in antisocial or violent behavior. There is a strong correlation between antisocial or violent behavior and drug use. Although a causal relationship is difficult to prove, research suggests that there is also a strong correlation between drug use and juvenile delinquency. Use of certain drugs, such as PCP and cocaine, is linked to increased aggression and violence. Many Mexican American high school dropouts encounter violence at home as well as within their peer groups. However, further research is needed to determine the specific relationship between drug use and violence among Mexican American youth.

Important research focusing on injection drug users (IDUs) sheds light on the complex dimensions of substance abuse within the Mexican-origin population. Mexican-origin IDUS have an increased chance of contracting and transmitting HIV and other blood-borne diseases. Their risk is higher because they are more likely to share needles and engage in risky sexual behaviors with partners who may or may not be IDUS.

Substance abuse issues have resulted in an increase in the number of drug-related emergency room visits among Hispanics. In addition, Mexican American youth have less knowledge about sex and HIV prevention than other groups, yet they are engaging in sex at similar rates. As Ernie, a health educator who works with Latino men, observed: "For a lot of these guys that may have a very *machista* attitude. They will not use condoms . . . that's part of the sexual power."

Understanding cultural nuances such as these is a necessity if we are to develop culturally competent drug abuse intervention programs that address AIDS prevention and education for this community. Again, these approaches must reflect and respect core cultural values such as familismo, **respeto**, and **confianza**.

Chapter 4 presents the problem of health care access for the nation's Mexican-origin population. Access is a major factor influencing health care decisions and treatment of illness. For Mexican Americans, barriers include **financial access** and access to culturally and linguistically competent care. The Mexican-origin population has a disproportionate number and percentage of people who are uninsured. More than one-third have no health insurance, either public or private. This occurs in part because many Mexican Americans have low-wage jobs with few fringe benefits, which prevents them from obtaining health insurance through their employers. Many of these workers are considered **working poor**. That is; they cannot afford private health insurance yet do not qualify for public programs such as Medicaid.

Other access issues unique to this population include the roles played by immigration and gender. Mexican immigrants comprise the largest sector of legal and undocumented immigrants in the United States, and they are highly concentrated in ethnic enclaves in the Southwest. Given their low-income status, they often must rely on publicly subsidized programs for their health and overall welfare needs. Unfortunately, the backlash from many whites against the growth of the Mexican-origin population in this region has created a hostile environment for this group, despite its enormous productivity in the workplace. This hostility is evidenced by the passage of California's **Proposition 187** in 1994, which prohibited the use of publicly subsidized health care services by undocumented immigrants. Although this law was challenged and modified, it nonetheless had a chilling effect on use of services by undocumented immigrants. In addition, Proposition 187 set the stage for further legislative discussions and initiatives aimed at limiting *legal* immigrants' use of publicly subsidized services.[1]

Another important distinction within the Mexican-origin population is women's access to health insurance. Susie eloquently expresses her access problems:

> I have a whole list of things that I need to do. I need to have an eye exam, I need to have a female checkup, I have to have a podiatrist look at my feet. Which they're fine, but it's part of the diabetic thing. . . . If I had insurance I would be able to go to the doctor and I'd be done. . . . My teeth are falling out of my head, literally. I don't go to the dentist because dentists want half of the money up front and I need thousands of dollars of work, but I'm terrified of the dentist. . . . It's a huge issue. (Susie D., 40)

Because many women rely on their spouses for health insurance, marital status is a major predictor of health insurance coverage. This is particularly true for Mexican-origin women because family obligations may interrupt their employment, and because they have limited employment opportunities available to them. Since many of these women are employed in the low-tier service sector, which includes jobs as domestics and child-care providers, they have limited opportunities to obtain private health care insurance. Moreover, because they often do not pay into the hospital insurance Part A trust fund (**Medicare**),[2] in their senior years they may find themselves ineligible for Medicare coverage. Lack of financial coverage for post-menopausal women between the ages of fifty and sixty-four is a serious issue. These women are at greatest risk of not having health insurance during a period when they are most likely to experience chronic diseases such as diabetes, hypertension, and breast cancer. The lack of health care can result in higher morbidity and mortality rates for this age group, which is outside the range most often studied in terms of the morbidity and mortality paradox.

A final and important dimension affecting health care access is the shortage of **bilingual** and **bicultural** health care professionals. Carmen illustrates the problem of obtaining quality health care in Tucson, Arizona, for her Spanish-speaking mother:

> The quality of care, the attention, the miscommunication [that her mother experienced] . . . there were times in her life when she needed to see a counselor. No one in the city of Tucson could find a bilingual counselor. And I know for a fact that there are bilingual counselors, but the doctors had no idea where to look. That's almost a crime to me because there is a whole population that is not getting proper health care. . . . I really think something needs to be done, especially in the Southwest, where the Spanish-speaking population is growing so rapidly, and it has been so predominant for so many years. (Carmen G., 49)

In order to develop culturally competent interventions and increase the availability of culturally sensitive sites of care, there must be an adequate pool of Mexican-origin physicians and other health care professionals. The current data illustrate that the percentage of health care professionals who are of Mexican descent is disproportionately small compared to the size of this group. However, programs have been started to address this problem. The Hispanic Centers of Excellence, for example, reach out to Hispanic students in kindergarten through twelfth grade, in order to expose them to the opportunities of medical school and other health-related career tracks. In addition, these programs, funded by the U.S. Department of Health and Human Services, provide support to students at the undergraduate and medical school levels to increase graduation rates. Without aggressive outreach, recruitment, retention, and intervention programs throughout the **educational pipeline**, the dearth of Hispanic health care professionals will continue into the mid-twenty-first century.

Chapter 5 discusses the importance of cultural values and **linguistic competency** in ensuring quality health care for the Mexican-origin population. Linguistic competency is defined as the availability of health care information in the language of the patient and the ability to communicate with patients in order to improve their health care. Providing linguistically competent care calls for added bilingual health care providers and professionals. Linguistic competency means more than translation or interpreter services, however. It is the first step in providing **culturally competent** care that meets the cultural needs of Spanish-speaking populations. A major factor to consider in providing linguistically and culturally competent health care services is Mexican folklore. Many of the illnesses perceived as diseases in the Mexican-origin community are rooted in the spiritual and folkloric domains of Mexican culture. Folklore illnesses may be treated with herbal remedies and spiritual practices such as *limpias* (ritual cleansings). These traditional remedies may either delay medical treatment of potentially serious illnesses or may complement medical treatment. Carmen's personal experience with folkloric remedies is described in the following vignette:

> There were always some *hierbas* (herbs) not far away. Herbs and home remedies have been part of my upbringing, so I believe in them a lot. . . . I've always tried acupuncture and energy healing and that sort of thing. And I'm a firm believer that they do work because they worked for me. (Carmen G., 49)

Health care professionals must be aware of culturally specific folkloric practices and beliefs as well as the use of alternative treatments, such as folk remedies, which may influence diagnosis and treatment of an illness. Although there is little evidence to confirm widespread use of alternative treatments within the Mexican-origin population, it is suspected that certain segments of the population make heavy use of them.

Ethnic, gender, regional, and class differences within the Mexican-origin community play important roles in defining ethnic and cultural identity, which in turn affects perceptions of disease and appropriate treatment. Therefore, to serve this population well, health care providers must be aware of these differences and cultural practices, as well as the degree of acculturation and biculturalism within the group they serve.

Medical personnel and staff can learn Spanish and achieve a measurable degree of linguistic competency, but learning cultural competency is more complex. In general, the best bridge between the Mexican-origin population and the health care system is through Mexican-origin health care professionals. This group, by virtue of life experience, should be the most culturally competent. María expresses her preference for Hispanic health care professionals this way:

> If I were to need a therapist for psychological reasons, I would prefer to have a Hispanic because they would understand me a heck of a lot better than any Anglo would. A lot of the issues that

we Hispanics have Anglos do not understand because of the culture. . . . I felt extremely comfortable with Dr. Duarte. . . . he was a Mexican, and there was a total comfort level with this doctor. . . . Somehow in my mind, I just felt that he understood. He understood where I was coming from, whatever issue it was, he seemed to be more sympathetic, he listened more, and was an excellent doctor. (María L., 44)

The unfortunate fact is that there are relatively few health care professionals of Mexican descent. Thus, it is incumbent on us to pursue a dual strategy of educating all health care professionals in the area of cultural competency while increasing the pool of qualified Hispanic health care professionals. As the Mexican-origin population in the Southwest and other parts of the country continues to grow, bettering its health and access to health care is vital to the overall health of the nation.

■ Interviewee Personal Profiles

The following people were interviewed in the course of preparing this book, in order to incorporate a sense of the everyday experiences of Mexicans and Mexican Americans in the U.S. health care system. All interviewees are of Mexican origin.

ENRIQUE ACUÑA JOY is a thirty-year-old Mexicano who was born in Hermosillo, Sonora, Mexico. He is a restaurant worker in Arizona.

LORENA BOJÓRQUEZ is a forty-eight-year-old Hispanic homemaker from Nogales, Sonora, Mexico.

SUSIE DUARTE is a forty-year-old Mexican American woman who was born in San Diego, California, and lives there today. She is a self-employed child care provider and has a degree from Santa Barbara City College.

■ Enrique Acuña

DANNY FLORES (not his real name) is a thirty-six-year-old Mexican American who was born in California. He is coordinator for an agency that provides services for at-risk teenagers. He currently resides in California with his family.

MARCO GÁMEZ is a twenty-eight-year-old Chicano from Agua Prieta, Sonora, who currently resides in Tucson, Arizona. He graduated from the University of Arizona in December 1999 with a major in Mexican American Studies and is planning to attend law school. Marco recently received his U.S. citizenship.

■ Marco Gámez

MARTÍN FABIÁN GÁMEZ is a thirty-one-year-old Mexican man who was born in Agua Prieta, Sonora, Mexico. He currently resides in Arizona and is employed by Motorola.

FRANCISCO GARCÍA, a thirty-five-year-old Mexican American physician, is an assistant professor of obstetrics and gynecology at University Medical Center in Tucson, Arizona. His current research focuses on cervical cancer screening along the U.S.–Mexico border.

■ Dr. Francisco García

CARMEN GASTELUM is a forty-nine-year-old Chicana from Nogales, Arizona, who has worked in Colorado as a financial services consultant. She currently resides in Tucson, Arizona.

MARÍA LOBATO is a forty-four-year-old Mexicana from Tijuana, Mexico. She currently resides in Tucson, Arizona, and is a case manager for dental and optical services at the St. Elizabeth of Hungary Clinic.

ANA MANZANO is a twenty-six-year-old Latina who was born in Tucson, Arizona. She currently resides in Tucson and is a bilingual second-grade teacher.

■ María Pacho

YOLANDA NIELBA is a fifty-two-year-old Mexican American woman who was born in Guadalajara, Jalisco, Mexico. She is an operator for Data Corporation.

MARÍA PACHO is a thirty-one-year-old Latina from East Los Angeles, California. She is the supervisor of the Youth Opportunity Movement program in the Los Angeles Community Development Department. Pacho has a master's degree in Public Health from Loma Linda University and received a bachelor's degree in Chicano/Latino Studies from Cal State Long Beach.

ERNIE PÉREZ, a forty-year-old Mexican American man, is a fourth generation Tucsonan. He is the current program manager for Salud y El Poder: The Latino Men's Health Project, which provides health education services to residents of Tucson and Sonora.

LILY QUIÑÓNEZ is a twenty-year-old Hispanic college student from El Paso, Texas. She is majoring in family studies at the University of Arizona.

MARISSIA QUIROGA is a twenty-two-year-old Mexican American nursing student from Santa Barbara City College. She is a part-time employee at St. Francis Hospital in Santa Barbara. She will be graduating in the fall of 1999 and plans to pursue her bachelor's degree.

REFUGIO ROCHÍN, a fifty-seven-year-old Mexican American man from Colton, California, holds a Ph.D. in agricultural economics.

■ Dr. Refugio Rochín

He is director of the Smithsonian Center for Latino Initiatives, which is part of the Smithsonian Institution in Washington, D.C.

GRACIELA (GRACIE) GUZMÁN SAENZ is a forty-six-year-old Mexican American lawyer from Houston, Texas, who specializes in international law and business transactions. Born and raised in Houston, Saenz was the first Mexican American woman to run for mayor of that city; she is also a former member of the Houston City Council.

■ Graciela Guzmán Saenz

■ Notes

1. After Proposition 187 and the changes in the federal welfare reform bill of 1996, there was significant discussion in Congress regarding limiting the right of legal immigrants to access health care programs such as Medicaid. The purpose of doing so was to discourage the legalization of low-income immigrants.

2. Either the woman or her husband must pay into the fund for forty quarters to be eligible for Medicare.

Mexican Americans & Health

"It was just an ideal location"

AN INTRODUCTION TO THE MEXICAN-ORIGIN POPULATION

My parents developed their business in community relations around provisions and Mexican food and supplies for small Mexican businesses. From the start, they instilled upon me the value of hard work, the value of being Mexican, providing products and services for the Mexican community. They also instilled upon me the importance of family. I cannot say my family ever hindered me. On the contrary, my family looks towards me as being special, encouraged me, and supported me in all activities I undertook, even though at times they didn't know what I was doing. Anytime I spoke to them, they always thought I was doing something new, different, and great. They were always very supportive. (Refugio R., 57)

My parents were always hard-working people. My father taught me work ethic. He was an individual that believed in work, and his philosophy of life [was], "If you work you don't starve. No matter how poor you may be, a good day's work you can do." He expected us to be up bright and early, and to be working constantly, and that's been my lifestyle ever since. (Gracie S., 46)

Refugio Rochín and Graciela Saenz represent both the diversity and strong work ethic that characterize many **Mexican Americans** in the United States. They are members of the country's largest **Hispanic** subgroup, and their roots are in the Southwest. One is the daughter of Mexican **immigrants**, the other a son of **native-born** Mexican Americans. Even though they share similar cultural backgrounds, they have their own unique histories. This convergence of cultural traits, individual identity, and common history forms the complex tapestry that is the Mexican American experience.

In this chapter, we will examine how individual health is intricately related to sociodemographic conditions. Because factors such as age, education, immigrant status, and occupation, as well as genetic factors, influence the risk of specific health problems, we will provide an overview of the **variables** (measurable elements) that affect the **health status** of the Mexican-origin population. These variables must be understood within the historical experience of this group in the United States. By framing these factors within their political geographic, historic, and economic context, we enhance our understanding of health problems affecting Mexican Americans and increase our chances of finding solutions to them. For example, the historical concentration of the Mexican-origin population in the nation's southern border region explains the current political-geographic location of the bulk of this group in the Southwest. We have divided this chapter into six sections: political-geographic concentration, historical factors influencing population growth and location, language status, educational level, occupational location, and concluding thoughts.

Political-Geographic Concentration of the Mexican-Origin Population

A major factor affecting the health status of Mexican Americans is where they live. The fact that they are concentrated in the Southwest results in regional influences that affect both the delivery and quality of health care. For example, Mexican Americans who live in the border region have a different quality of health care than those in urban areas such as Chicago. While inequalities may exist in both locations, different political and institutional environments affect the health care systems in various states and regions. Another important factor is whether Mexican Americans are a significant percentage of both the general and Hispanic populations of a state or region, as this too will set the cultural context in which we recommend health policies.

The Mexican-origin population makes up more than 60 percent of the entire Hispanic population of the United States. Almost 84 percent of Mexican-descent individuals reside in the southwestern states of Arizona, California, Colorado, New Mexico, and Texas—with California and Texas accounting for 74 percent of the total. Since 1980, however, the fastest rates of growth have been occurring in unlikely places such as New Jersey, Delaware, and Alaska. Midwestern **metropolitan areas** such as Chicago

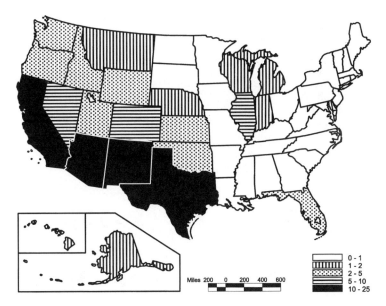

■ Figure 1. Mexican American Population as a Percentage of Total Population, 1990

Legend:
- 0 - 1
- 1 - 2
- 2 - 5
- 5 - 10
- 10 - 25

Miles 200 0 200 400 600

have long had significant Mexican-origin populations as well. Thus, the growth of this Hispanic **subpopulation** within the last twenty years has been rapid and has reached beyond the Southwest.

The current growth of the Mexican-origin population relative to the **non-Hispanic** population in the Southwest can be attributed to two major factors: (1) a higher **fertility rate** in the Mexican-origin population, and (2) immigration. The maps in figures 1 and 2 illustrate the size of the Mexican-origin population by state and the growth of that population from 1980 to 1990.

Table 1.1 shows the percentage of Mexican-origin people within each of the southwestern states relative to the state's overall Hispanic population. Based on the 1990 U.S. census, the two states with the largest concentration of Mexican-origin Hispanics relative to other Hispanic subpopulations are Texas and Arizona. People of Mexican origin represent more than 90 percent of the total Hispanic population of these two states. Thus, border states with long international boundaries have the highest concentration of Mexican-origin people within their overall Hispanic populations. As the southern borders of Texas and Arizona together account for more than 1,600 miles of the U.S.–Mexico border, it is not surprising that they contain significant points of entry for Mexicans coming into the United States.

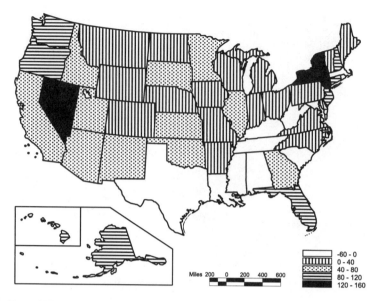

Miles 200 0 200 400 600

-60 - 0
0 - 40
40 - 80
80 - 120
120 - 160

Figure 2. Percentage Change in Mexican American Population, 1980–1990

The concentration of Mexican Americans in the border region has unique health implications. First, the rapid population growth on both sides of the U.S.–Mexico border has placed great pressure on the limited public health infrastructure of this area. As a result border residents are at greater risk of exposure to infectious diseases as well as environmental hazards. Second, both the U.S. border population and the Mexican border population are politically isolated from their respective federal governments. Therefore, they have limited ability to influence the reallocation of government resources to the border region. Thus, health issues may be ignored or health services may be underfunded until a catastrophic health event occurs.

California has the largest number of Mexican-origin people, with more than six million. Many of the Mexican-origin residents of California are newcomers, as California, like New York, is a magnet for various immigrant groups. This is partly due to California's rich employment base, **ethnic enclaves** that provide kinship relationships to recent immigrants, and a relatively generous public infrastructure that assists immigrants in integrating into mainstream American society. In addition to the large Mexican-origin population in California, other Hispanic groups, such as Guatemalans and Salvadorans, are well represented. These groups are

Table 1.1 Mexican Americans as a Percentage of the Total Hispanic Population in Each Southwestern State

STATE	TOTAL HISPANIC POPULATION IN STATE	PERCENTAGE OF MEXICAN ORIGIN
Arizona	1,410,052	93.4
California	10,113,156	83.8
Colorado	572,256	71.3
New Mexico	738,534	60.4
Texas	6,544,218	92.6

Source: Interview with Arturo González, assistant professor, University of Arizona Mexican American Studies and Research Center, June 8, 2000.

located within, or in close proximity to, Mexican-origin communities. More than 50 percent of California's Hispanic population resides in just five of its fifty-two counties: Los Angeles County, Orange County, San Bernardino County, Riverside County and San Diego County. These southern counties, which stretch from the border north to Los Angeles, reflect the uneven concentration of the Mexican-origin population within the state.

Colorado and New Mexico also have relatively large Mexican-origin populations. New Mexico, however, is uniquely characterized by its sizable **Hispano/a** population, with deep roots that well precede statehood and, in some instances, are linked to Spanish colonial times.[1] Thus, many New Mexicans define their identity more as Hispano/a or Nuevo Mexicanos than as Mexican Americans. Although the case of Hispanos/as in New Mexico is interesting, they represent a small proportion of the total U.S. Mexican-origin population.

In Arizona, almost one in four residents is of Mexican origin, and in California the figure reaches almost one in three. In Texas and New Mexico the ratio is one in three. Underlying the present immigration and fertility trends are many historical factors that have influenced the geographic concentration of this group in the Southwest. The proximity of the U.S.–Mexico border provided an entry point for earlier immigrants and continues to be an entry point for more recent ones. Yet the historical legacy of Spanish and Mexican settlement patterns predates current national boundaries. Spain, and later Mexico, had control of this area for more than a century before it was lost to the United States. This early history is the initial basis for the settlement patterns of the Mexican-origin population.

Table 1.2 Foreign-Born versus Native-Born Mexican-Origin Population in the Southwest, 1990

STATE	NATIVE-BORN (%)	FOREIGN-BORN (%)
Arizona	75	25
California	57	43
Colorado	88	12
New Mexico	85	15
Texas	76	24

Source: U.S. Census Bureau, *1990 Census of Population: Social and Economic Characteristics, Arizona, California, Colorado, New Mexico, Texas* (Washington, D.C.: Government Printing Office, 1990).

Another important trend is the rapid growth of the **foreign-born** Mexican-origin population, particularly in California (see table 1.2). This can be attributed to the significance of Mexico as an immigrant-sending country. It is also a result of the Immigration Reform and Control Act (IRCA), which allowed immigrants who had lived continuously in the United States without legal documentation since before January 1, 1982, to legalize their status between the time of the law's passage in 1986 and May 4, 1988. As the vast majority of these immigrants were of Mexican origin, IRCA disproportionately affected the status of Mexican immigrants. The majority of these newly legalized immigrants resided in two states: California and Texas.

 ## Historical Concentration of the Mexican-Origin Population

The roots and kinship ties that were established when the U.S. Southwest was part of Mexico are the basis for a disproportionate concentration of Mexican-origin people there. Much of what is now known as the American Southwest was Spanish territory (New Spain) for three centuries prior to Mexican independence in 1821. After Mexico became an independent nation, a significant segment of its territory was in the path of a rapidly expanding United States. A key turning point in the history of the U.S.–Mexico borderlands took place in 1848. This date marks the end of the brief but bitter U.S.–Mexican war, which drastically altered the geographic boundaries of both countries. As a result of this war, Mexico lost a gigantic portion of its territory, which had included the present-day U.S.

states of California, Arizona, New Mexico, Texas, Utah, Nevada, and parts of Colorado, Wyoming, Oklahoma, and Kansas. In 1853, the **Gadsden Purchase** changed the boundary again to include within the United States additional portions of present-day New Mexico and Arizona. The year 1848 also marks the important **Treaty of Guadalupe Hidalgo,** which ended the U.S.–Mexican war. It defined, among other things, the property and civil rights of the Mexican and Hispano/a population in the territory ceded by Mexico to the United States.[2] The following maps (figures 3 to 6) illustrate the shifting political boundaries of the American Southwest and show how, despite U.S. westward expansion, Hispanic roots remained deeply embedded in the political, social, and historical traditions linked to Mexican and Spanish culture.[3]

The deep cultural roots are linked to the political-geographic settlement patterns of many Mexican Americans, as illustrated by the experience of Carmen Gastelum:

> My mother's side of the family came from Sonora—Hermosillo— and my father's family came across on a French ship. They mixed up with the Seri Indians and came north with the Yaqui Indians until they came up to Arizona before it was the U.S., and settled in the Santa Cruz Valley.

Knowing the history of the Mexican-origin population, particularly in the Southwest, is important because it helps us understand current migration flows and ethnic concentrations. This knowledge also helps put into context the current tensions within the Mexican-origin community over land rights, identity, and marginalization from the power structures of American society. In addition to recognizing landownership, the Treaty of Guadalupe Hidalgo guaranteed that individuals who lived within the Mexican territory ceded to the United States would be given full political rights as U.S. citizens and that their civil rights would be protected. Unfortunately, U.S. federal and state governments failed to honor and comply with the treaty's requirements after the war, reflecting the escalating negative sentiments toward Mexicans that further fueled ethnic and racial divisions within the Southwest.[4] These historical and political factors influence how Mexican Americans enter the health care system and how they are treated within it.

Given this historical context we can begin to understand the pervasiveness of conflict between the dominant non-Hispanic power structure and

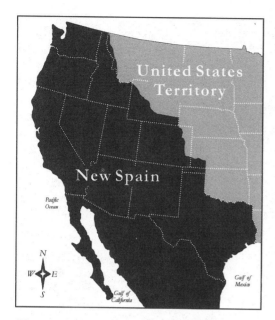

Figure 3. Border between New Spain and the United States, 1800–1819

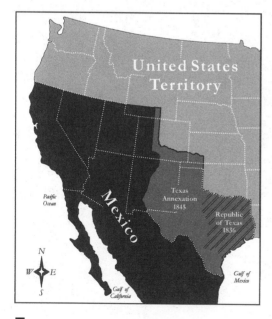

Figure 4. Border between Mexico and the United States, 1819–1848

the Mexican-origin population over land, language, and equity issues. Notwithstanding this conflict, Mexican settlement in the southern border region continues. Today, growth in border regions and ethnic enclaves of the Southwest affects both the Mexican-origin and larger non-Hispanic communities. According to historian Oscar Martínez, the borderland milieu has enormous implications for a nation. "The expansion of economic activity in a border zone means population growth at the margin of the nation and consequent migration . . . across the boundary. Finally, questions of national identity emerge as borderlanders fuse their culture with that of their neighbors, creating new social patterns that people in the heartland zones may find abhorrent."[5] Thus, new tension points emerge as Mexican nationals increasingly migrate beyond the border, influencing both the cultural and sociodemographic composition of American society. These tensions are exacerbated by the resiliency and growth of the Spanish language in the border region as well as in large cities such as Los Angeles and Houston, where recent Mexican immigrants have become the dominant group. Such population growth and cultural shift in the urban core of the Southwest has created growing concern over how health care resources should be delivered and used.

Language Status

> Well, actually I'm bilingual, so it's been great. If I wasn't bilingual, there would definitely be a problem. . . . I'm talking in Spanish and English [at work]. . . . You definitely need to be bilingual. (María L., 44)

Many of the central issues of Mexican-origin identity and economic status within the broader U.S. society are framed within the context of the Spanish language. Today many health care professionals realize that Spanish language fluency is a critical skill for providing quality service to the Mexican-origin population. Language constitutes a symbolic component of ethnic identity for many

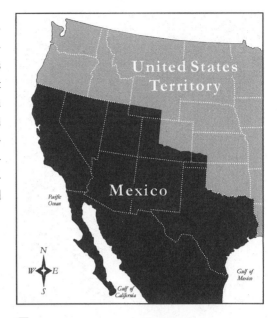

Figure 5. Border between Mexico and the United States, 1821

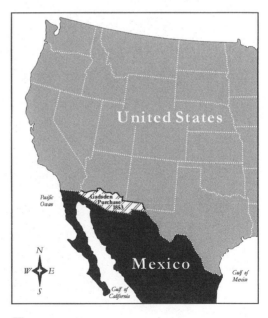

Figure 6. Border between Mexico and the United States, 1848–Present

members of this group. Spanish is inextricably linked to Mexican identity, and often it is difficult to separate the two. Thus occurs what Margarita Hidalgo identifies as the "Spanish Mexican equation," which highlights an interesting contradiction: the Spanish language is sometimes viewed as an asset, and at other times as a liability. In the former case, Spanish links the individual to the home culture, and in the latter case it excludes the individual from mainstream U.S. society.[6] The Mexican-origin community often experiences an internal conflict that manifests itself in the struggle to maintain the Spanish language while striving for economic assimilation into American society. In most instances, economic assimilation requires English skills and fluency, yet this fluency may result in a loss of the familial language. For some Mexican Americans this loss is viewed as a betrayal of one's own ethnic roots, given the historical context in which Mexicans were punished socially and economically for speaking Spanish. At the same time, many Mexican-origin families who live outside the border region have less exposure to Spanish-speaking recent immigrants. For them the decline of Spanish language use and eventual language loss may occur naturally through the process of intergenerational change and assimilation into U.S. society. This division between cultural assimilation and intergenerational progress, given the historical reality of language discrimination, has created for many a need to symbolically resist English immersion and retain the Spanish language as an essential part of one's Mexican identity. This resistance is best illustrated in the recent passage of California's Proposition 227, which eliminated bilingual education in public schools. Many Mexican American leaders in the state lobbied against this initiative based on their fear that it was racially motivated as it targeted primarily Spanish-speaking Mexican immigrants. Thus, this proposition galvanized the Spanish-speaking community for two reasons: because of a common ethnic identity that is heavily tied to language and because of continued concern over institutionalized discrimination by the state.

There is now evidence of a reverse language shift in some Mexican ethnic enclaves, particularly in the border region. Reverse language shift occurs when Spanish supersedes English as the dominant language.[7] Unfortunately, this does not occur without a backlash from some members of the dominant society, who view widespread Spanish use as "un-American." An excellent example of this backlash occurred when the city council of the Texas border town of El Cenizo decided to conduct its monthly meetings in Spanish. This decision was based on providing greater access to the government for the citizens, most of whom speak Spanish. In fact, Spanish is the dominant language in El Cenizo. This local decision created a national uproar that was fomented by talk show hosts and nativist groups opposed to bilingualism. The hostility is best illustrated by the following excerpt from nationally syndicated radio talk show hosts Don Geronimo and Mike O'Meara during an on-air interview with one of El Cenizo's town commissioners, Flora Barton.

BARTON: We speak Spanish to the people that do not understand English.

DON: Get on your burro and go back to Mayheeco! . . . If those people do not understand my language, they should get on their burros and go back to Mayheeco.

BARTON: You have to understand that if someone speaks Spanish, that does not make them un-American or any less of an American.

DON: You people have your own country. Why are you trying to ruin our language?[8]

The reaction to the language policy of El Cenizo graphically illustrates the existing racism toward Mexican-origin people. In this case, Spanish is symbolic of the perceived threat that Mexican culture poses to the dominant way of life. On the other hand, El Cenizo town leaders recognized that to effectively deliver public services such as health care, the dominant town language, Spanish, has to be used.

In spite of the white backlash originating in non-border areas of the United States, the Spanish language has resiliency because of the continual influx of Mexican immigrants. Moreover, many health care systems in the region are now requiring that their providers have some degree of fluency in Spanish. In the Southwest, significant portions of the Mexican American population may be characterized as bilingual. As illustrated in table 1.3, with the exception of Colorado, more than 70 percent of all Mexican-origin individuals are bilingual. Moreover, in the two largest southwestern states, approximately 40 percent of the Mexican-origin population does not speak English well. Thus, for a major portion of the Mexican-origin population in the Southwest language fluency will continue to be an important issue.

Beyond the historical and symbolic dimensions of language, social science research clearly indicates that English language fluency is a key to

Table 1.3 English Language Ability of Mexican-Origin People in Five Southwestern States (Five Years of Age or Older)

STATE	SPEAK LANGUAGE OTHER THAN ENGLISH (%)	DO NOT SPEAK ENGLISH "VERY WELL" (%)
Arizona	74	30
California	77	43
Colorado	48	19
New Mexico	73	26
Texas	85	40

Source: U.S. Census Bureau, *1990 Census of Population: General Population Characteristics* (Washington, D.C.: Government Printing Office, 1990).

educational and economic mobility in the United States. An extensive body of literature indicates that English language skills and proficiency play an important role in the educational and economic success of Mexican-origin people. Moreover, subtle differences in language fluency such as grammatical skills, accented English, and conversational fluency are important predictors of income and socioeconomic status for Mexican-origin persons in the United States.[9] Without English fluency, **educational attainment** is severely constrained and prospects for economic mobility are limited. Lack of fluency also impedes effective communication in the sphere of social services such as health care. The significance of the latter point is illustrated by Jill Reichman's study, in which she states that for many Mexican Americans, regardless of English ability, Spanish is the native language and therefore the "language of illness and somatic [bodily] distress."[10] Thus, the issue of language use includes a practical component that affects the employment and health status of many people.

■ Educational Level

> To me, education is so important because it will make me a better person. I am going to learn something that I will be able to use for the rest of my life. Not only that, it's going to help me make decisions that will help me to succeed and make more money to [be] financially set when I [am] at an age where I can no longer work. (Martín G., 31)

When I was growing up my father always used to say that we could graduate, as girls we could graduate up to high school, but afterwards he expected us to work and contribute to the family. To him, there was no need for me to go to college, 'cause I would probably just get married, have kids, and there would be no need for it. And so his understanding of the role of the woman was very difficult or very different from what was actually taking place in the U.S. My father had actually been raised in Mexico and came to the U.S. as an adult, so his understanding of the role of [women], how he thought he should raise us as women was a conflict in my life, and a real struggle. (Gracie S., 46)

Educational attainment is another important factor influencing the health status of the Mexican-origin population. Level of education influences the occupational status of Mexican-origin people in all parts of the United States; occupational status in turn predicts whether or not they will rely on public or private health care services. Education also influences the extent to which individuals are aware of risky behaviors or of predisposing conditions that may influence their own health. For example, in states such as California and Texas, where there are large Mexican immigrant populations, almost 20 percent of the Mexican-origin population twenty-five years and older has less than a fifth-grade education. In the other southwestern border states, with the exception of Colorado and New Mexico, less than 50 percent of the Mexican-origin population within this category has a high school diploma, and less than 10 percent has a baccalaureate degree (see figure 7).

Education status among this group is a hotly debated issue because of three observable trends. First, the Mexican-origin population has one of the highest high school dropout rates and one of the lowest college completion rates in the nation. Second, educational policies such as bilingual education—which were created to improve educational attainment and rectify past discrimination against language-minority students—are currently under public scrutiny and attack. Finally, given the increasingly globalized and high-skill-based U.S. economy, continued poor academic performance may result in further socioeconomic segregation.

The failure of America's public schools to educate the Mexican-origin population adequately is rooted in segregation. Institutionalized, or **de jure**, segregation of this group in southwestern schools occurred between 1900 and 1950, and **de facto segregation** (segregation that exists but is not

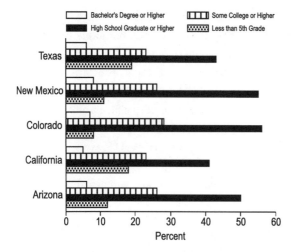

Legend:
□ Bachelor's Degree or Higher   IIIII Some College or Higher
■ High School Graduate or Higher   ▒▒▒▒▒ Less than 5th Grade

Texas
New Mexico
Colorado
California
Arizona

0   10   20   30   40   50   60
Percent

■ Figure 7. Educational Level of the Mexican-Origin Population, by State (Age 25 and Older) (*Source:* 1990 Census of Population, General Population Characteristics, table 120: Arizona, California, Colorado, New Mexico, and Texas)

supported by law) still occurs.[11] In light of the educational discrimination against the Mexican-origin population in the Southwest, community leaders developed educational policies and programs to address both linguistic and cultural differences. The first of these programs was bilingual education, which was enacted into law in 1968 during the Nixon administration with the passing of the Bilingual Education Act.

The importance of bilingual education cannot be overstated; it was the first attempt to rectify systematic discrimination in the public schools against the Mexican-origin population based on linguistic differences. These programs have been successful in addressing linguistic discrimination, but issues of adequate funding and implementation continue to plague them. Moreover, a key to the success of any school-based program is having a continuous enrollment of students. Although bilingual education was critical in rectifying past educational discrimination, the shift in the demographic profile has limited the implementation and success of these programs. That is, the Mexican-origin population is now made up of more immigrants and is more mobile compared to the more-established Mexican-origin population of the 1960s. This is particularly true in states such as California.

In reality, bilingual education alone cannot address the complexity of educational issues facing Mexican Americans. Individual characteristics such as immigration status and English language skills, as well as household characteristics such as parental education and poverty levels, are important predictors of educational success. These factors further complicate the use of specific strategies such as bilingual education in addressing educational attainment problems. Future education policies will need to address these factors if they are to be successful.

■ Occupational Location

Educational attainment is directly linked to **occupational location**, which refers to the type of job and economic sector in which a person is employed. Therefore, educational attainment and educational policy ultimately have critical implications for the economic success of Mexican Americans. Because occupational location is a critical factor in determining **health care access** and influencing health status, it is important to develop a general economic portrait of the Mexican-origin population. For example, Mexican Americans who are employed in low-tiered jobs such as farm labor are at greater risk for job-related injuries such as pesticide poisoning.

Overall, the distribution of Mexican Americans in the U.S. economy is largely concentrated in lower-tiered blue-collar and service employment. In the Southwest, a significant portion of the Mexican-origin population is still employed in agriculture. For example, in Arizona, almost one in five Mexican-origin workers is employed in agriculture. In California, a state that is heavily dependent on agricultural production, about one in ten is employed in agriculture (see figures. 8 through 12).

Racial discrimination also influences the employment of many Mexicans within the Southwest. Perhaps no sector in the U.S. economy captures this historical reality as profoundly as the agricultural sector, due to three main factors: (1) the early dominance of agricultural interests in developing this labor market; (2) the recurring shortage of low-skilled labor in this sector, given the wages and working conditions; and (3) the ideological need of federal and state officials to racialize labor market policies to justify unequal wage and working conditions for fieldworkers. The last point is important as historically it allowed for the exclusion of agricultural workers from key legislation influencing the degree of collective bargaining in this market. This prevented farmworkers from unionizing sooner, which also limited their access to health insurance. In addition, immigration policy was flexible with respect to migrant seasonal workers, allowing for a continuous flow of low-wage Mexican labor to the agricultural fields of the Southwest. Such policies contributed to a **racialized** labor market in the region that further limited the political participation of Mexican immigrants in the debates over national and state health policy.

Racialized labor markets systematically placed Mexican-origin workers in specific segments of employment and wage categories. This practice was common in the major sectors that employed Mexican workers for most of

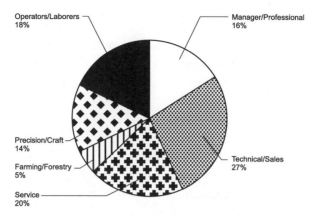

Figure 8. Occupations of Mexican-Origin People: New Mexico (*Source:* 1990 Census of Population, Social and Economic Characteristics, table 124, New Mexico)

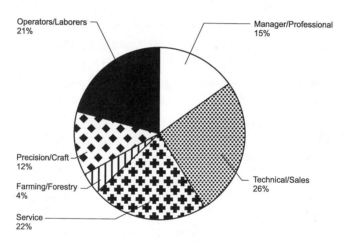

Figure 9. Occupations of Mexican-Origin People: Colorado (*Source:* 1990 Census of Population, Social and Economic Characteristics, table 124, Colorado)

the twentieth century, such as agriculture, ranching, mining, railroads, and the industrial blue-collar and service industries. As scholar Mario Barrera has noted, "Occupational stratification remained an even more marked characteristic of the urban labor system in the first three decades of the century, as data for several major cities make clear."[12]

Many farmworkers still have no means of obtaining quality health care or related services, even though they face disproportionate exposure to work-related health hazards such as direct contact with pesticides and

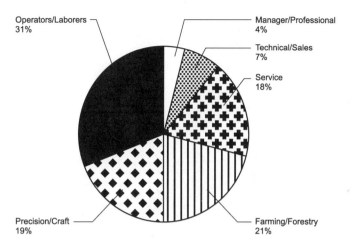

Operators/Laborers 31%
Manager/Professional 4%
Technical/Sales 7%
Service 18%
Precision/Craft 19%
Farming/Forestry 21%

■ Figure 10. Occupations of Mexican-Origin People: Arizona (*Source:* 1990 Census of Population, Social and Economic Characteristics, table 124, Arizona)

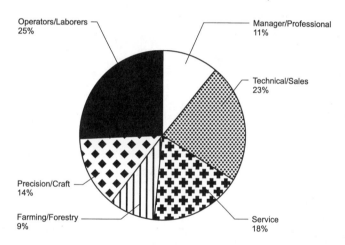

Operators/Laborers 25%
Manager/Professional 11%
Technical/Sales 23%
Precision/Craft 14%
Farming/Forestry 9%
Service 18%

■ Figure 11. Occupations of Mexican-Origin People: California (*Source:* 1990 Census of Population, Social and Economic Characteristics, table 124, California)

other toxic chemicals that cause illness or even death. The mainstream environmental movement had recognized the danger of pesticide exposure as a valid concern by 1960. However, it was not until 1965 that the plight of farmworkers, especially those in California, finally received widespread attention with the help of farm labor activist César Chávez. Between 1965 and 1971, the campaign for farmworkers' rights, fair wages, and better living conditions also challenged health and environmentally related civil rights violations such as pesticide exposure.[13]

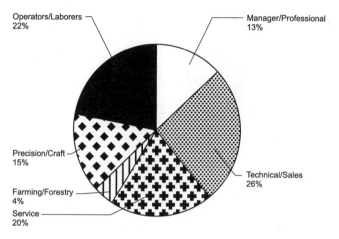

Operators/Laborers
22%

Manager/Professional
13%

Precision/Craft
15%

Farming/Forestry
4%

Service
20%

Technical/Sales
26%

■ Figure 12. Occupations of Mexican-Origin People: Texas (*Source:* 1990 Census of Population, Social and Economic Characteristics, table 124, Texas)

Exposure to pesticides is just one of the many occupational health hazards that plague Mexican-origin workers. Their overrepresentation in blue-collar and manual-labor jobs places them at higher risk for exposure to work hazards, which in turn affects their overall health status. Workers are often unaware that they have been or are being exposed to harmful materials, such as pesticides, and therefore do not report incidents to company superiors or health care professionals. They rarely recognize that many chronic health problems and illnesses are work related or are caused by prolonged exposure to chemicals and an unsafe work environment.[14]

Although agriculture is no longer the dominant sector for Mexican-origin workers, their continuing employment in low-tier service and blue-collar jobs contributes to the creation of problems similar to those of the past. Further, because of their overrepresentation in low-wage jobs, many are isolated in poor ethnic enclaves (neighborhoods) where environmental hazards are also frequently present.

Figures 8 to 12 illustrate the dominant sectors of employment for Mexican-origin workers in five states of the Southwest. These charts highlight the occupational categories that influence the health status profile of this population. Notwithstanding the current debates on immigration restrictions, the demand for low-wage Mexican immigrant workers continues to relegate these workers to the lowest occupational segments of the U.S. economy. This has direct implications for the health of Mexican workers and that of their families. As is the case with agricultural workers, these lower-tiered jobs pose greater risks of work-related injuries, unsafe working conditions, and environmental hazards. Adding to the risk of such jobs is that they are less likely to offer health insurance.

■ Concluding Thoughts

This chapter has highlighted the relationship between the political-geographic location of the Mexican-origin population and its present health status. Both have been influenced by the history of what is today the American Southwest. Discrimination and segregation in schools and the labor market have contributed to present-day inequalities in health care. The location of Mexican-origin communities is important because it influences language proficiency in English and Spanish, as well as educational and occupational opportunities, thus affecting the health of community members. In addition, social networks in established ethnic enclaves largely influence immigrant settlement patterns. These boundaries ultimately influence the cultural milieu of this group, its social and work environments, and its access to health care.

This chapter also provides an overview of selected sociodemographic variables that influence the present-day health status of the Mexican-origin population. Among these variables are language, education, immigrant status, and occupation. In addition, it is possible to expand and refine these predictors by including variables such as marital status, family size, age, and income level. These broad characteristics provide a basis for understanding the factors underlying health care access, environmentally related health issues, and cultural and linguistic beliefs and behaviors. Genetic factors also play an important role, which will be explored in the next chapter.

■ Discussion Exercises

1. What factors should be considered in defining the health status of the Mexican-origin population? What indicators can be used to measure health status?

2. How has the historical experience of Mexican Americans affected their geographic concentration, language use, and the formation of ethnic enclaves?

3. Discuss the links between variables such as language, education, and occupation and the socioeconomic status of the Mexican-origin population in the United States.

4. How has continuous Mexican immigration affected the overall status of the U.S. Mexican-origin population in terms of language, culture, education, and health status?

5. How has legislation directed toward the Mexican-origin population affected their legal status and access to education and health care services? Consider the Treaty of Guadalupe Hidalgo, the Bilingual Education Act, and IRCA.

6. How are Spanish language and ethnic identity connected? What are different ways in which these concepts are constructed and perceived within and outside of the Mexican American community?

7. How does the concentration of Mexican-origin workers in certain sectors of the U.S. economy affect earnings, working conditions, and health risks?

■ Suggested Readings

González, G. G. *Chicano Education in the Era of Segregation.* Philadelphia: Balch Institute Press, 1990.

Griswold del Castillo, R. *North to Aztlán: A History of Mexican Americans in the United States.* New York: Twayne Publishers, 1996.

——. *The Treaty of Guadalupe Hidalgo: A Legacy of Conflict.* Norman: University of Oklahoma Press, 1990.

Gutiérrez, D. G. *Walls and Mirrors.* Berkeley: University of California Press, 1995.

Hamamoto, D., and R. Torres. *New American Destinies: A Reader in Contemporary Asian and Latino Immigration.* New York: Routledge, 1997.

Hispanic Americans: A Statistical Sourcebook. Boulder: Numbers and Concepts, 1991.

Martínez, O. J. *Border People: Life and Society in the U.S.–Mexico Borderlands.* Tucson: University of Arizona Press, 1994.

Pulido, L. *Environmentalism and Economic Justice: Two Chicano Struggles in the Southwest.* Tucson: University of Arizona Press, 1996.

Romero, M., P. Hodagneu-Sotelo, and V. Ortiz. *Challenging Fronteras.* New York and London: Routledge, 1997.

San Miguel, G. *"Let All of Them Take Heed": Mexican Americans and the Campaign for Educational Equality in Texas, 1910–1981.* Austin: University of Texas Press, 1987.

Tienda, M., and L. Jensen. "Immigration and Social Program Participation: Dispelling the Myth of Dependency," *Social Science Research* 15 (1986), pp. 372–400.

U.S. Department of Commerce, Economics and Statistics Administration, Bureau of the Census. *We the American Hispanics.* Washington, D.C.: Government Printing Office, 1993.

Vélez Ibáñez, C. G. *Border Visions: Mexican Cultures of the Southwest United States.* Tucson: University of Arizona Press, 1996.

■ Notes

1. S. Rodríguez, "The Hispano Homeland Debate Revisited," *Perspectives in Mexican American Studies* 3 (1992), p. 98. Inclusion of Hispanos/as in the Mexican American ethnic group is widely accepted, even by those who support this group's claim to cultural uniqueness. According to Rodríguez, "none of the principals seem seriously to be denying that Hispanos are Mexican Americans."

2. O. J. Martínez, *Border People* (Tucson: University of Arizona Press, 1994), pp. 27–33.

3. The maps are compiled from the following sources: Martínez, *Border People;* L. M. Metz, *Border: The U.S.–Mexico Line* (El Paso: Mangan Books, 1989); J. J. Wagoner, *Arizona: Its Place in the United States* (Salt Lake City: Peregrine Smith Books, 1989) and *Arizona's Heritage* (Salt Lake City: Peregrine Smith Books, 1987); and A. Wexler, *Atlas of Westward Expansion* (New York: Facts on File, 1995).

4. D. Gutiérrez, *Walls and Mirrors* (Berkeley: University of California Press, 1995), pp. 17–18, 20.

5. Martínez, *Border People,* p. 25.

6. M. Hidalgo, "Language and Ethnicity in the 'Taboo' Region: The U.S.–Mexico Border," *International Journal of the Sociology of Language* 114 (1995), p. 31.

7. Ibid.

8. "Excerpts from Don and Mike's Messages of Hatred to Hispanics," *Hispanic Link Weekly Report* 17, no. 34 (August 30, 1999), p. 3.

9. See A. Dávila, A. K. Bohara, and R. Saenz, "Accent Penalties and the Earnings of Mexican Americans," *Social Science Quarterly* 74, no. 4 (December 1993), pp. 902–15; or K. E. Espinosa and D. S. Massey, "Determinants of English Proficiency among Mexican Migrants to the United States," *International Migration Review* 31, no. 1 (Spring 1997), pp. 28–50.

10. J. S. Reichman, "Language-Specific Response Patterns and Subjective Assessment of Health: A Sociolinguistic Analysis," *Hispanic Journal of Behavioral Sciences* 19, no. 3 (August 1997), p. 358.

11. According to a 1999 study by Orfield and Yun, Latino/a segregation in the public schools continues to occur in areas where there is a large Latino/a or Spanish-speaking population, and this experience is similar to that of African Americans. See G. Orfield and J. T. Yun. "Resegregation in American Schools," The Civil Rights Project, Harvard University, web site: http://www.law.harvard.edu/civilrights/publications/resegregation99.html.

12. M. Barrera, *Race and Class in the Southwest: A Theory of Racial Inequality* (Notre Dame, Ind.: University of Notre Dame Press, 1979), pp. 76–89.

13. L. Pulido, *Environmentalism and Economic Justice: Two Chicano Struggles in the Southwest* (Tucson: University of Arizona Press, 1996).

14. Ibid.

"It's about having a healthy body"

THE HEALTH STATUS OF
MEXICAN AMERICANS

Hispanics now make up the largest ethnic minority group in the United States, particularly in the Southwest. Yet it is very troubling to find that there is still relatively little information on the **health status** of the overall group or the four major Hispanic subgroups (**Mexican Americans,** Central and South Americans, Puerto Ricans, and Cubans). One may well ask how the U.S. government or individual states can make informed health policy decisions regarding Hispanics when there is such a paucity of knowledge. In this chapter, we highlight what is known about the health status of Mexican Americans and discuss changes that need to be made in order to meet the health care needs of this large group.

The Historical Context of Health and Disease

To understand contemporary Mexican American concepts of disease and healing, we must first examine the historical context of several core indigenous (native) beliefs and their **syncretism,** or merging, with those of the colonial Spanish. The Indians of Mesoamerica,[1] influenced primarily by the Mixteca or Aztecs, believed in three animistic forces (multiple souls) that have relevance in contemporary Mexican folk medicine.[2] According to Ortiz de Montellano (1990), in Mesoamerican culture, a person's health depended on the relative amounts of each soul at a given time and on the maintenance of balance among them. *Tonalli,* believed to be located in the head, provided a vital hot force. It imparted bravery, vigor, and warmth, and made growth possible. Involuntary loss of one's Tonalli could cause illness or even death. *Teyolia,* believed to be located in the heart, provided vitality, knowledge, and vocational ability. The Aztecs believed the heart to be the center of thought and personality. This soul, unlike Tonalli, could be separated from the body only at the time of death, and was known as the soul "that goes beyond after death." The third animistic force was *Ihiyotl*. Thought to be located in the liver, Ihiyotl provided vigor, passions, and feelings such as desire, envy, and anger. Sins, particularly of a sexual nature, were believed to harm the liver and make it emit Ihiyotl, which could harm others. The Aztecs believed health to be holistic. To stay healthy one had to be in equilibrium, do things in moderation, and perform one's duty. States of illness and health were closely related to a condition of equilibrium or disequilibrium. Health required a person to maintain equilibrium physically, in social relations, and with the deities. Causes of disease included supernatural (religious), magical, and natural (physical) causation, but all were intertwined. The Aztecs had their own system of "hot" and "cold" diseases, similar to but different in important ways from the Spanish model.

The Spanish brought with them to the Americas concepts of disease and healing based on **Hippocratic-Galenic beliefs**, and to some extent, concepts derived from Arabic medicine. A major part of this belief system was the existence of four humors, or liquids, in the body—black bile, yellow bile, phlegm, and blood. The relative levels of the humors in a person's body determined his or her temperament and physical and mental characteristics, as well as having the potential to cause disease. Additionally, given the pervasive belief in witches and witchcraft during the sixteenth century, the Spanish also believed in the supernatural causation of disease through hexes and spells. The most important concepts derived from the Spanish were the concepts of "hot" and "cold" diseases derived from Hippocratic-Galenic medicine. Vasodilation (opening of the blood vessels) and a high metabolic rate characterized "hot" diseases, whereas vasoconstriction (narrowing of the blood vessels) and a low metabolic rate characterized "cold" diseases. Examples of "hot" conditions include pregnancy, hypertension, diabetes, acid indigestion, **susto**, **mal de ojo**, and **bilis**. Examples of "cold" conditions include menstrual cramps, pneumonia, colic, **empacho**, and **frío de la matriz**. "Cold" remedies usually treat "hot" diseases and "hot" remedies usually treat "cold" diseases.

It is important to keep this historical perspective in mind when examining the health status of Mexican Americans. In particular, contemporary concepts of illness and wellness are closely linked to several aspects of historical beliefs, especially in terms of the common folk illnesses found among Mexican Americans.

The Sociocultural Basis of Health and Disease

> I do have to say that I believe that it [language] definitely had to have been an issue when I was growing up because we did live in poverty, but my grandparents were never on welfare or any kind of assistance. . . . [N]ow that I think back, they didn't consider looking into those options. I'm sure that we would have definitely qualified because we had a house full of children. (María L., 44)

Health does not exist in isolation from socioeconomic or cultural factors. In fact, socioeconomic status profoundly influences health status, both positively and negatively. Cultural values, beliefs, and attitudes influence help-seeking behaviors. There is no question that income, **educational attainment**, and poverty levels are closely linked to health. Mexican Americans as a group have lower incomes, lower educational attainment, and higher poverty rates than **non-Hispanic** whites. But how exactly do these socioeconomic differences affect health status?

Several socioeconomic characteristics of the Mexican-origin population have a harmful effect on both its general health care behaviors and its general health status. Low income, substandard housing, inadequate or unsanitary living facilities, lack of formal education, ethnic segregation and discrimination, poor nutrition, and stress can and do affect the health of Mexican Americans in a number of ways. Overcrowded housing and lack of appropriate sanitation increase exposure to infectious diseases. Low education levels result in decreased awareness of health promotion and disease prevention activities (such as diet, exercise, reducing risk of exposure to diseases). Additionally, these barriers limit utilization of health care and prescription medications, and contribute to institutionalized racism and discrimination. Finally, they increase the probability that an individual will choose alternative forms of health care that may be ineffective or even harmful. Many diseases found among the Mexican-origin population are associated with poverty. Bacterial and parasitic diseases and tuberculosis, for example, are related to overcrowding, poor nutrition, and inadequate housing and sanitation.

> When I found out that my uterus had fallen and tipped, I was told by someone that maybe I could get massaged and that they could lift it up. . . . Everybody wants to try to avoid any type of surgery at

all costs and if there is another alternative that you have heard about then you kind of want to give it a try. . . . I had gone to a *santero* [spiritual healer], I was taking a friend, and while he was there [I] decided to go ahead. I asked him if he felt it was a good idea to have the surgery and he said it wasn't and he is the one that suggested for me to seek someone that could massage and put it back. (María L., 44)

Cultural influences also affect Mexican American health and health care behavior. Cultural values such as **machismo** among men and **marianismo** among women influence decisions to seek health care, symptom recognition, and disease management. Cultural values such as **familismo, personalismo, confianza, dignidad**, and **respeto** affect the provider-patient relationship, and help determine whether a patient stays in treatment or follows prescribed regimens. Cultural beliefs regarding health and illness shape how a person communicates individual health problems, perceives and interprets symptoms, chooses when and where to go for care, decides how long to stay in care, and evaluates the care received.

Perhaps the most widely examined cultural concept in relation to the health status of Mexican Americans is **acculturation**. Acculturation is a dynamic process. It signifies dual learning and the blending of mainstream (European American) cultural values, beliefs, attitudes, and behaviors with those originating in Mexican culture. Acculturation is often measured by indicators such as language preference and use (Spanish or English), ethnic identification (Mexican, Mexican American, **Chicano/a**, or Mexicano/a), birthplace (Mexico or the United States), and generational status (first, second, or higher order).[3] Acculturation is believed to influence behaviors, attitudes and beliefs, and values held by members of the Mexican-origin population. Using this concept health researchers have found that less acculturated Mexican-origin individuals tend to have inaccurate health information and lack relevant health knowledge regarding symptom recognition. At the same time, research has also shown that more acculturated Mexican Americans tend to have poorer nutrition and engage in more health-related risk behaviors such as use of tobacco, alcohol, and drugs. However, a major problem with this concept is that greater acculturation is often associated with higher educational and income levels (both of which are known to influence general health status), as well as access to and use of health care services. Therefore, given that persons of lower socioeconomic status are also more likely to be less acculturated (and vice versa) it is necessary to disentangle the effects of socioeconomic status and acculturation level.

 ## Health Promotion and Disease Prevention in the Mexican American Community

> At eighteen years old . . . doctors detected my illness and noticed that my illness was spreading and not stopping. The illness had reached my kidneys. I had weighed one hundred pounds, and my kidneys stopped functioning. I went through very hard times due to the symptoms of my illness. I was not able to do anything on my own, and my family helped me. . . . It was very hard, we spent about ten years paying medical bills. (Lorena B., 48)

The development and implementation of health promotion and disease prevention programs in Mexican-origin communities are critically needed. However, to develop such programs we need a thorough understanding of the **epidemiological** (distributional) factors that contribute to disease, the cultural factors that weaken or enhance disease prevention, and the socioeconomic profile of the community to be targeted.

Researchers have suggested several acculturation models to explain variations in disease **incidence** and **prevalence**. (The two most common measures of disease rates, incidence and prevalence refer, respectively, to the number of new cases of a disease and the total number of cases of a disease.) The majority of these models relate health outcomes to **acculturative stress,** the stress of adapting one's culture to the mainstream culture.[4] The "simple acculturation" model proposes that acculturation is not in itself stressful and therefore is not associated with increased incidence or prevalence of disease. The "acculturative stress" models suggest two opposite outcomes: either less acculturated Hispanics, because of their health values and health behaviors, will show higher incidence and prevalence of disease than more acculturated Hispanics; or alternatively, more acculturated Hispanics, due to cultural loss, will show higher incidence and prevalence of disease than less acculturated Hispanics. The "**bicultural**" model suggests that Hispanics who retain traditional cultural values and behaviors while also being able to interact with the dominant culture will have better health status than both poorly and highly acculturated Hispanics.

In spelling out causal factors, it is important to understand key epidemiological concepts such as incidence, prevalence, **relative risk**, and **attributable risk**. (Very generally, relative risk measures the likelihood that members in a group will contract a disease, and attributable risk measures the number of illnesses caused by exposure to a disease.) It is also critical to know which risk factors contribute to specific diseases and what the prevalence of these risk factors is in the Mexican-origin community. For example, cardiovascular disease (heart disease and heart attack) is the leading cause of **mortality** (death) among Mexican American adults. Several important **modifiable risk factors** contribute to the incidence of cardiovascular disease, such as high cholesterol levels, smoking, lack of exercise, and **obesity**. Research shows that these risk factors are more prevalent among Mexican Americans than non-Hispanic whites. This information helps to target the behaviors that contribute to these risk factors.

Cultural factors that weaken or enhance disease prevention efforts include gender role concepts such as machismo and marianismo, cultural beliefs regarding effective cures and treatments, and cultural values or attitudes about the body and the disease itself. For example, breast cancer is the leading cause of mortality among Mexican American women. Yet the cultural value of marianismo dictates that a woman should place the health care needs of other family members before her own. Fear and anxiety about cancer may act as another barrier to early screening. Cultural values related to avoidance of touching the body or allowing someone else to view or touch the body (even a health professional) may prevent some Mexican-origin women from performing breast self-exams, agreeing to clinical breast exams, or obtaining a mammography.

One of the most widely used public health models of disease prevention includes the concepts of **primary, secondary**, and **tertiary prevention**. Each of these levels of prevention is directly linked to the **natural history of disease**. The natural history of disease has four stages: susceptibility (risk factors), pre-symptomatic disease (signs of disease begin to appear), clinical disease (recognizable signs and symptoms of disease are present), and disability (reduced function or impairment occurs). Primary prevention focuses on addressing modifiable risk factors in the susceptibility stage to prevent the disease from progressing. The ultimate goal of primary prevention is to reduce incidence (number of new cases) of a disease. Secondary prevention targets individuals who are beginning to show pre-symptomatic or symptomatic signs of disease. They receive services such as early detection and risk-reduction education designed to slow or stop the progression of the disease. The goal of secondary prevention is to reduce the prevalence of disease (the total number of people affected by a disease). Lastly, tertiary prevention focuses on those individuals who have the disease in its full clinical stage, resulting in some disability. The goal of tertiary prevention is to restore health and reduce the level of disability caused by the disease.

Socioeconomic factors are important because they contribute to the incidence and prevalence of disease, as well as providing us with information on which subgroups to target and in what form intervention should be delivered. For example, imagine that a community assessment finds that the majority of Mexican-origin people living in a particular area are monolingual Spanish speakers and have low literacy rates in both Spanish and English. These factors mean that one must present the risk-reduction message in Spanish and through media outlets that do not depend on reading ability.

Understanding epidemiological factors, cultural factors, and socioeconomic factors is just the beginning. These factors must now be used to develop culturally competent health promotion and disease prevention programs targeting Mexican Americans. (For a thorough discussion of **cultural competency**, see chapter 5.) Here we will briefly highlight important elements needed for the development of culturally competent interventions that focus on risk reduction.

The placement of the health promotion/disease prevention program is critical. That is, it must occur in a geographic setting that is accessible and acceptable to Mexican Americans. Clearly, the program must be community-based, i.e., set within the Mexican-origin community. Care must be taken to ensure that the **subjective culture** (attitudes, values, beliefs, etc.) of Mexican Americans is well represented.[5] The program must be staffed with bicultural and **bilingual** individuals. Client-staff interactions must be guided by core Mexican and Mexican American cultural values such as **simpatía**, personalismo, dignidad, respeto, and confianza. Depending on the specific disease and modifiable risk factors targeted, concepts such as familismo, religiosity, and spirituality may play roles as well.

An essential component of any prevention program is community empowerment, or strengthening the community's ability to meet its own needs. One model that encompasses this underlying goal is the Nuestro

Bienestar model developed by the Center for Health Policy Development in San Antonio, Texas. This model is guided by **razalogía**, a community development approach originating in the 1970s.[6] According to Andrade and Doria-Ortiz, "The razalogía model takes as its mission the empowerment of *raza* communities, and it challenges each individual community member to identify, contrast and compare, and then reject concepts and behaviors which weaken their resolution to act on behalf of the community's *bienestar* (health, well-being, strength, unity)."[7] Other aspects of community empowerment include having an advisory board composed of community members and obtaining a consensus from the community on the importance of targeting specific risk factors or diseases. A useful guide to follow when developing an intervention is Freire's problem-posing method. This method involves having community members identify the problem, analyze its causes, and develop solutions.[8]

 ## The Health Status of Mexican American Subgroups

> We did live in a poor area, and when my dad left we became poorer. My dad left when I was seven, so after seven years old when the electricity went out, we used candles. When there was no food, we didn't eat. When the window broke, it stayed broke. When our car broke down, it stayed in the parking lot. Things just stayed bad and they didn't get better. . . . It was really hard for me to believe that anything was ever going to change in my life. I used to wonder when my dad was going to come home, wonder when days would change and when life was ever going to get better. It got a lot worse before it ever got better. (Danny F., 36)

Children and Youth

The health of Mexican American children and youth is inextricably linked to the socioeconomic and cultural factors affecting their parents and families. A useful heuristic (problem-solving) approach is to examine the socioeconomic, institutional, and cultural contexts that influence the health of children and youth, acknowledging that all three contexts are interrelated.[9]

The socioeconomic context includes factors such as poverty, educational attainment, and median household income. As noted in chapter 1, a significant number of Mexican-origin families live below the **federal poverty level**. In 1996, one-fourth of all Hispanics were living in poverty, which was three times the rate of non-Hispanic whites. Further, almost two-thirds of Hispanic children (those eighteen years of age and younger) were living in or near poverty.[10] This proportion increases when only female-headed households are considered, showing that approximately 89 percent of Hispanic children in this situation were living in poverty in 1996. The fact that higher rates of poverty are found among female-headed households than in other household types is referred to as the "**feminization of poverty**." The educational attainment of parents is another important factor that may harm or aid the health of children and youth. Among Hispanics twenty-five years of age or older, 70 percent have less than twelve years of education, and it is well established that income increases with educational attainment. Results from the 1997 Current Population Survey show that median household income for Hispanics increases threefold with number of years of education.[11]

The institutional context of health involves many of the factors identified in the next chapter concerning **health care access**, the ability to obtain and pay for health care. Some of the more important factors include health insurance coverage, having a regular source of care or a particular provider, and barriers to health care use.

Data collected as part of the Hispanic Health and Nutrition Examination Survey (HHANES)[12] show the following rates for Mexican American adults: 34.1 percent of men and 33.9 percent of women did not have health insurance coverage; 35.1 percent of men and 17.8 percent of women did not have a regular source of health care; 42 percent of men and 30.7 percent of women did not have a particular provider; and 33 percent of Mexican Americans reported encountering one or more barriers when last attempting to obtain health care. Among those encountering barriers, 73 percent reported that the barrier(s) were serious enough to prevent them from obtaining health care.

Clearly, parents of Mexican American children are at a distinct disadvantage relative to non-Hispanic whites in reference to the institutional context of health care. Other factors, such as California's **Proposition 187** (which attempted to prohibit undocumented immigrants from obtaining publicly funded health care), not only limit access to health care for undocumented Mexican **immigrants**, but also serve to institutionalize discriminatory practices by health care facilities. These discriminatory practices present barriers to legal immigrants and native-born Mexican Americans as well as undocumented immigrants.

The cultural context of health among Mexican American children and youth involves familial cultural practices and values that either promote health or detract from it. Mexican-origin families often have hierarchical family roles, extended family systems, and gender role expectations. Mexican-origin children usually acculturate or adapt to the U.S. mainstream society more quickly and easily than their parents. Consequently, there may be more intergenerational conflict between parents and children in terms of appropriate gender and age-specific roles. Additionally, because many Mexican American families have more than one child in the home, an older child may be expected to care for younger ones and to assist parents in their acculturation to mainstream society. This can result in the "parentification of children." That is, too much responsibility is placed on youth without additional familial support or guidance. The effects of these stressors can lead to mental health and substance abuse problems as youths mature.

Emergent Health Issues for Mexican American Children

Several important health issues affecting Mexican-origin children are highlighted in this chapter; they are underimmunization, obesity, and oral health.

> [T]he issue of transportation was a big issue. My mother depended upon social service agencies, charitable hospitals. . . . she depended on the sisters of charity to obtain health care for all of us. [For] immunizations we had to go to the clinics. . . . [W]e would walk to the clinic. We would have to traverse railroad tracks, busy intersections, and she had all these kids, and we just had to stick together as much as possible. My mother was very determined; even though it was difficult to access, she never failed to . . . get us necessary immunizations and so forth. (Gracie S., 46)

The underimmunization of Mexican American children is probably the most fundamentally important health issue they face. Lack of needed immunizations may prevent them from being enrolled in school, but more importantly it contributes to increased communicable disease incidence, prevalence, and **morbidity** (rate of illness). Most childhood communicable diseases are preventable with appropriate immunization. In 1996, only 71 percent of Hispanic children nineteen to thirty-five months of age had been vaccinated for the combined series of diphtheria-tetanus-pertussis (DTP) vaccine, polio vaccine, measles-containing vaccine, and Haemophilus influenzae type b (Hib) vaccine.[13] Hispanic children living in poverty had significantly lower vaccination rates than those living at or above the poverty level: 65 percent versus 72 percent, respectively. Underimmunization is an even greater problem in the U.S.–Mexico border area. Available evidence from the HHANES shows that only 61 percent of Mexican American children ages six to eleven years had the age-appropriate number of DTP immunizations.[14] The low level of childhood immunizations among Mexican Americans reflects a number of underlying issues: lack of knowledge regarding immunization efficacy, lack of health care access, and lack of affordable health care.

Obesity, being significantly overweight, is another important indicator of the future health status of Mexican-origin children and youth. Obesity is a primary modifiable risk factor for the development of diabetes, heart disease, cerebrovascular disease (stroke and high blood pressure), and cancer. Available data indicate that Mexican American children are significantly more overweight than non-Hispanic white children. For example, 18.8 percent of Mexican American boys ages six to eleven years were overweight, compared to 14.6 percent of non-Hispanic white boys of the same age. Moreover, 15.8 percent of Mexican American girls ages six to eleven years were overweight compared to 11.7 percent of non-Hispanic white girls of the same age.[15] Obesity and above-average weight are risk factors that can be lessened through increased exercise and better nutrition.

Oral health is another important issue affecting Mexican-origin children. In general, Hispanics have higher rates of periodontal (gum) disease than non-Hispanic whites. Periodontal disease such as gingivitis (redness and swelling of the gums) is very prevalent among Mexican American children. A study on oral health found that slightly more than three-fourths of Mexican American children five to seventeen years of age had gingivitis.[16] The levels of tartar and plaque in Mexican-origin children were higher than those of Cuban American children but lower than those of Puerto Rican children. These findings point to future trends of tooth decay, tooth loss, and severe periodontal disease among Mexican Americans as they age.

Mexican American Adolescents

> I would say that the use of drugs and alcohol . . . has bothered me ever since I was going to school. I could possibly have respiratory problems because I have smoked quite a lot . . . marijuana was what I smoked the most. (Enrique A., 30)

> My mother . . . left to go take care of her mom when I was fourteen. . . . I never wanted to be in a gang and I never wanted to use drugs or alcohol. . . . There was substance abuse in my house. There was violence and it became a hopeless place, and a lot of my friends started using and I never wanted to use. (Danny F., 36)

Mexican-origin adolescents engage in a number of risk behaviors that may be detrimental to their present and future health status as well as their future socioeconomic status. Again, the social, cultural, and institutional context of health makes an important contribution to understanding the health status of Mexican American adolescents. One can readily see that the same issues that influence children's health also affect the health of adolescents.

Diabetes is a metabolic disorder that results from the body's inability either to convert glucose into energy due to lack of insulin (Type I diabetes) or to adequately use the insulin produced (Type II). As a consequence, glucose builds up in the blood, which can lead to a diabetic coma. The prevalence of Type II diabetes (**non-insulin-dependent diabetes mellitus** or NIDDM), which is often triggered by lifestyle factors such as poor diet and obesity, is increasing among Mexican Americans. Part of this increase is due to the early onset of NIDDM among Mexican American adolescents.[17] Neufeld and colleagues found 45 percent of incident cases (new cases) of NIDDM among youth in one provider setting. Modifiable risk factors for diabetes include obesity and being overweight, high dietary fat and low fiber intake, and a sedentary lifestyle.[18] All of these factors are reportedly higher in Mexican American adolescents than non-Hispanic white adolescents.

Early sexual activity and teen pregnancy are other important issues facing Mexican American adolescents. Adolescence is a time of rapid physiological maturation. Mexican American girls reach puberty sooner than non-Hispanic white girls. This earlier age of menarche, when females begin their menstrual period, is a factor in both the higher **fertility rate** found among Mexican Americans and the higher teen pregnancy rate. Available research suggests that even though Mexican American girls have a lower reported rate of sexual activity in comparison to non-Hispanic white girls, they tend to use contraceptives less.[19] This puts them at greater risk for pregnancy, which may affect continued growth and development. It also places them at risk for sexually transmitted diseases such as HIV/AIDS, human papillomavirus (HPV), syphilis, gonorrhea, trichomonas, and chlamydia. Lack of contraceptive use by both adolescent Mexican American boys and girls can certainly lead to unintended pregnancies and a life of low socioeconomic status resulting from dropping out of school or the inability to find well-paying jobs.

Motor vehicle accidents, homicides, and suicides are leading causes of death among all adolescents, including Mexican-origin teens. While the mortality rates for motor vehicle accidents are similar to those of non-Hispanic whites, Mexican American adolescents have a higher prevalence of homicide and suicide deaths. The homicide rate among Hispanic adolescents is almost five times higher than that of non-Hispanic whites.[20] Hispanic adolescents are also more likely than non-Hispanic white adolescents to report at least one suicide attempt in the past year.[21]

Mexican American Adults

As Mexican Americans move from adolescence into adulthood a number of changes in cellular structures of the body and organs have taken place. Most of these changes are directly attributable to lifestyle behaviors during adolescence. This section will briefly highlight key morbidity and mortality characteristics of Mexican American adults.

MORBIDITY AND MORTALITY

If a person doesn't have health insurance, they don't have access to a provider. . . . Unless they really know what's really going [on] with the community . . . if they don't have proper insurance they're not going for their preventative health exams so that'll hinder someone [who] is developing some type of disease. It is not going to be caught on time. They'll probably be diagnosed with later stages of the disease like my mother. . . . she was diagnosed with breast cancer at her later stages, it wasn't at a point where it could be caught [i.e., arrested]. So if a person doesn't have health insurance and they're not going for their routine health physicals then a person will become sicker. (María P., 31)

The general health status of Mexican American adults is correlated with educational level and income. For example, among Mexican Americans forty-five to sixty-four years of age with less than twelve years of education, 30 percent rated their health as fair or poor compared to only 15 percent of those with twelve years or more of education.

Chronic diseases are directly related to illness, hospitalization, and limitation of activity. Among Mexican-origin adults, major chronic diseases include NIDDM, heart disease, stroke, cancer, and HIV disease.

NIDDM is one of the more prevalent diseases found among Mexican Americans; it is the seventh leading cause of death among Hispanics, non-Hispanic whites, and African Americans. However, the nature of NIDDM means that it is often a contributing factor in deaths due to heart disease and kidney failure.

The most important factor is to have early detection for your health. . . . [A]fter I was pronounced with diabetes I wasn't having a yearly checkup and worrying about how do I feel. I learned through my experience with my illness that you have to have a yearly checkup. . . . [N]ow my main goal is not to go on insulin. So it depends on my diet, on my medication, and my monthly blood test. (Yolanda N., 52)

It is estimated that one of every ten Mexican Americans over twenty years of age has diabetes.[22] Results from the Third National Health and Nutrition Examination Survey (NHANES III) support this. Data from this survey show that the prevalence of diagnosed diabetes is 9.3 percent for Mexican Americans compared to 4.8 percent for non-Hispanic whites. The prevalence of undiagnosed diabetes is 4.5 percent for Mexican Americans compared to 2.5 percent for non-Hispanic whites. Thus, the prevalence of both diagnosed and undiagnosed diabetes among Mexican Americans is two times higher than among non-Hispanic whites. The prevalence of diabetes also increases with age. The prevalence of diabetes was 24 percent for Mexican Americans forty-five to seventy-four years of age.

Recent evidence from the Centers for Disease Control and Prevention

(CDC) Behavioral Risk Factor Survey suggest that both the prevalence of NIDDM and risk factors for its development are high for southwestern Hispanics compared to non-Hispanic whites.[23] The prevalence of obesity among Hispanics residing in the five southwestern states of Arizona, California, Colorado, New Mexico, and Texas ranged from a low of 15.9 percent (Colorado) to a high of 24.9 percent (Texas). The prevalence of NIDDM in the five southwestern states ranged from a low of 5.3 percent (New Mexico) to a high of 8.2 percent (Texas).

Risk factors for diabetes include obesity and being overweight, impaired glucose tolerance, insulin resistance, and a family history of diabetes. The prevalence of obesity is higher among Mexican Americans than non-Hispanic whites, which contributes to the higher incidence of diabetes. Also, overweight Mexican-origin women have a higher risk for the development of diabetes during pregnancy than overweight non-Hispanic white women. The prevalence of diabetes among Mexican Americans whose parents have diabetes is twice as great as for Mexican Americans with no family history of diabetes. Impaired glucose tolerance is higher among Mexican Americans than non-Hispanic whites. The NHANES III reported a prevalence rate of 13.8 percent among Mexican Americans compared to 10.3 percent among non-Hispanic whites.[24] Two population-based studies have demonstrated higher insulin levels among Mexican Americans than non-Hispanic whites.[25] These higher insulin levels may reflect resistance to insulin reception in tissues due to increased adiposity (fat content), and are predictive of NIDDM incidence.

Complications resulting from late diagnosis and poor medical management of NIDDM are also more prevalent in Mexican Americans than non-Hispanic whites. The prevalence of proteinuria, a key indicator of kidney damage, is more common among Mexican Americans, and the rate of diabetic retinopathy, an eye disease often leading to blindness, is more than twice that of non-Hispanic whites. Additionally, Mexican Americans with NIDDM have a higher rate of peripheral vascular disease (damage to the blood vessels), leading to amputation of the feet or legs, than is found in non-Hispanic whites. Taken together, the increasing incidence and prevalence of NIDDM will lead to premature death among Mexican Americans if it is not detected early and appropriately managed. The key to reducing the incidence of NIDDM among Mexican Americans is to target modifiable risk factors—obesity and being overweight—through increased exercise and better-quality diets. Persons with a known familial history of diabetes should obtain appropriate screening for diabetes. By reducing incidence, we can also reduce the prevalence of NIDDM.

Cardiovascular disease includes heart disease, congestive heart failure, and myocardial infarction (heart attack). Heart disease is the leading cause of death among all racial/ethnic groups in the United States. Cerebrovascular disease includes hypertension (high blood pressure) and stroke and is the sixth leading cause of death among Hispanics.[26] Major contributing factors to the incidence of cardiovascular and cerebrovascular diseases include atherosclerosis (hardening of the arteries), obesity, being overweight, high cholesterol, poor diet, a lack of exercise, cigarette smoking, family history, and NIDDM.

Atherosclerosis is the underlying condition for both cardiovascular and cerebrovascular disease. It occurs when the inner layers of the artery walls become thickened by a buildup of fatty deposits and other substances. As the inner wall of the artery thickens, there is less space for the blood to flow through, resulting in a diminished blood supply. Symptoms of reduced blood flow include chest pain and hypertension. A stroke results when an artery in the brain is either ruptured or clogged by a blood clot (thrombus), a wandering clot (embolus), or atherosclerosis plaque. Cells in the affected region of the brain die within minutes, resulting in disability. Bleeding in the brain caused by an aneurysm (weakening and ballooning of a blood vessel) is the other principal cause of stroke. This type of stroke is the result of a ruptured blood vessel that bleeds into the brain tissue (called cerebral hemorrhage).

Research has shown that Mexican Americans and non-Hispanic whites have similar prevalence rates of elevated cholesterol and slightly higher rates of hypertension. For example, the NHANES II found the prevalence of elevated cholesterol to be 20 percent and 19 percent among Mexican American men and women, respectively, compared to 19 percent and 20 percent among non-Hispanic white men and women. The rate of hypertension was found to be 19 percent and 17 percent among Mexican American men and women, respectively, compared to 24 percent and 21 percent among non-Hispanic white men and women. Nevertheless, deaths due to coronary heart disease are significantly higher for Mexican Americans than for non-Hispanic whites. The mortality rate for heart disease is 956.2 per 100,000 for Mexican American men ages sixty-five to seventy-four, compared with 917.5 per 100,000 for non-Hispanic white males of the same age. Additionally, Mexican Americans have greater hospitalization rates, in-hospital death rates, and general death rates when compared to non-Hispanic whites.[27] This may be a result of factors such as cultural beliefs, a failure to recognize symptoms, or a lack of access to health care. A study from the National Institutes of Health (NIH) found that Mexican Americans are hospitalized for heart attacks more often than non-Hispanic whites. Further, the highest heart attack rates were found among Mexican American men, followed by non-Hispanic white men, Mexican American women, and non-Hispanic white women.[28]

> As we all know, stress is the causing factor for many diseases. . . . I developed pretty large fibroids in my uterus and as a result I had to have a hysterectomy because I was losing a lot of hemoglobin and I became acutely anemic in the process, to the point where I had to have a transfusion because of it. (Carmen G., 49)

Cancer is the second leading cause of death among Hispanics. The three most common types of cancers found in Mexican-origin men are lung cancer, cancer of the prostate, and colon cancer. The three most common types of cancer found in Mexican-origin women are breast cancer, lung cancer, and colorectal cancer. The incidence of lung cancer among Mexican American men and women is approximately 25 and 10 per 100,000, respectively, which is about 45 percent lower than for non-Hispanic white men and women. The five-year survival rates for lung cancer are about 9 percent for Mexican American men and 15 percent for Mexican American women, which are similar to rates for non-Hispanic whites. The major risk factor for lung cancer is cigarette smoking, which accounts for 87 percent of the attributable risk.

The colorectal cancer incidence rates for Mexican-origin men and women are 25 and 21 per 100,000, respectively, which again is lower than for non-Hispanic whites. Colorectal cancer incidence rates are about 25 percent lower for Mexican Americans than non-Hispanic whites. However, five-year survival rates are slightly lower for Mexican American males than for non-Hispanic white males (41 percent compared to 46 percent) and are similar for Mexican American and non-Hispanic white females (50 percent). The major risk factors for colorectal cancer are a low-fiber, high-fat diet; low intake of fruits and vegetables; physical inactivity; a family history of colorectal cancer; or a history of polyps and inflammatory bowel disease.

Among Mexican-origin men, prostate cancer has an incidence of 70 per 100,000, slightly lower than that of non-Hispanic white males. The five-year survival rate for prostate cancer is also slightly lower for Mexican Americans than non-Hispanic whites, approximately 72 percent compared to 78 percent, respectively. Causes of prostate cancer are largely unknown, but some research suggests that occupational exposure, a diet high in fat, early sexual activity, an increase in sex hormones, and a family history contribute to the incidence of prostate cancer.

> There were complications due to the loss of blood that I had prior to surgery and during surgery and then when I first was able to get in, the doctor requested was not the doctor I saw. . . . I got a referral to see a gynecologist and again with him I waited for about an hour and saw him for five minutes and I was really concerned because I didn't feel that he took time to get to know my case and who I was. (Carmen G., 49)

Aside from colorectal cancer, the two most prevalent cancers found among Mexican-origin women are breast cancer and lung cancer. Mexican American women have a significantly lower incidence rate of breast cancer than non-Hispanic white women, 50 per 100,000 compared to 72 per 100,000, which is about 29 percent lower. However, five-year survival rates were slightly lower for Mexican American women in comparison to non-Hispanic white women, 72 percent versus 75 percent, respectively. The major risk factors for breast cancer include first-term pregnancy after age thirty, obesity after menopause, alcohol consumption, high-fat diet, lack of physical activity, and family history. The major risk factor for lung cancer is the same as that for men, as described on the previous page.

One of the chief methods for achieving lowered incidence and prevalence of all the common cancers found among Mexican Americans is early detection through appropriate screening. Although this appears to be an easy solution, numerous sociocultural factors interfere with achieving it. These include a general lack of knowledge about recognizing symptoms and effective treatments, lack of health care access and use of preventive health services, and attitudes and values regarding the human body, especially those areas most affected by these cancers—the breast, cervix, and prostate.

Data from the 1987 National Health Interview Survey showed that 16 percent of Mexican American women aged eighteen or older had never heard of or had a **Pap smear** compared to only 2 percent of non-Hispanic white women.[29] Additionally, 38 percent of Mexican American women aged eighteen or older had never heard of or had a mammogram. Both of these exams are critical to the early detection and treatment of cervical and breast cancer. Thirty-eight percent of Mexican American men and 47 percent of Mexican American women aged forty or older had never had or heard of a digital rectal exam (to detect colorectal cancer), compared to just 20 percent and 17 percent of non-Hispanic white men and women, respectively. Clearly, knowledge of cancer screenings must increase among Mexican Americans in order to reduce the incidence and prevalence of these major forms of cancer.

The **human immunodeficiency virus** (HIV), which causes acquired immunodeficiency syndrome (AIDS), is the fourth leading cause of death among Hispanics. The **epidemiology** of HIV disease among Mexican Americans is similar to that for non-Hispanic whites but very different from that for Puerto Ricans. HIV is transmitted through unprotected sexual intercourse, transfusions of infected blood, and the sharing of drug-injection paraphernalia. A study from the CDC shows various transmission categories for different Hispanic subgroups.[30] Among Mexican-born males, 68 percent contracted the virus through male-male sex, 6 percent through injection drug use, 6 percent through male-male sex and injection drug use, and 3 percent through heterosexual contact. In contrast Puerto Rican males acquired the virus primarily through injection drug use (61 percent). Mexican-born women acquired the virus in two primary ways: sex with an HIV-positive male (36 percent) and transfusions (33 percent). Subdividing the cases of sexually transmitted HIV in women, sex with an HIV-positive male accounted for 19 percent, followed by sex with an injection drug user (11 percent), and sex with a bisexual male (6 percent). Seven percent of Mexican-born women acquired HIV through injection drug use. Again, this is in stark contrast to Puerto Rican women who acquired the virus primarily through injection drug use (46 percent), sex with an injection drug user (35 percent), and sex with an HIV-positive male (6 percent). Among non-Hispanic white women, 42 percent acquired HIV through injection drug use, 17 percent through transfusions, 17 percent through sex with an HIV-positive male, and 6 percent through sex with a bisexual male. Unfortunately, there are a number of misconceptions regarding HIV transmission among Mexican Americans, including the idea that it can be contracted from mosquitoes and casual forms of contact. Equally unfortunate is the fact that sexuality is usually not discussed openly within the Hispanic culture, which makes it difficult to implement successful prevention programs. Clearly, in dealing with sexuality cultural sensitivity is especially important.

Estrada compared and contrasted the sexual risk behaviors of Puerto Ricans and Mexican Americans. Behaviors under study included history of sexually transmitted diseases (STDs), number of sexual partners, and frequency of condom use.[31] The results appear in table 2.1. No differences were found in the number of sexual partners between Mexican Americans and Puerto Ricans. As can be seen, slightly more Mexican Americans were at immediate risk than Puerto Ricans. The common Mexican American attitude about sex and HIV is described by Ernie, who works with **Latino** men in Tucson, Arizona:

> The more [power] you have sexually, the more machista you are, the most satisfied you are with being the macho, the image of el hombre. But . . . there's also that part where you are at risk of either being infected or not knowing that you are infected and infecting others. And many of these men, they downplay having to use condoms for safe sex or [say] that they don't want to get tested because they are not in that group of people who do get HIV, and that's . . . one of the attitudes of our people, "If I'm not a drug user or if I'm not gay, I can't get the disease because I'm a man and I'm married and that's how it is." (Ernie P., 40)

RISK FACTORS FOR CHRONIC DISEASE   By and large, the prevalence of risk factors for the major chronic diseases discussed previously are lower among Mexican Americans than non-Hispanic whites. Mexican Americans have lower serum cholesterol levels, a lower prevalence of cigarette smoking, and a lower prevalence of hypertension than non-Hispanic whites. The only exception is for obesity. Approximately 31 percent of Mexican-origin men are overweight in comparison to 24 percent of non-Hispanic white men. Similarly, approximately 42 percent of Mexican-origin women are overweight in comparison to 24 percent of non-Hispanic white women. There is no question that the lower prevalence of key risk factors for heart disease, stroke, and cancer contribute to the lower mortality rates for these diseases among Mexican Americans in comparison to

Table 2.1 Sexual Risk Behaviors of Two Hispanic Subgroups

	PUERTO RICAN (%)	MEXICAN AMERICAN (%)
History of STD(s)	29	18
Always use condom	14	7
SEXUAL RISK INDEX RATING:		
Low risk	58	47
Intermediate risk	18	24
High risk	24	29

Source: A. L. Estrada, "Drug Use and HIV Risks among African American, Mexican American, and Puerto Rican Drug Injectors," *Journal of Psychoactive Drugs* 30, no. 3 (1998), pp. 247–53.

non-Hispanic whites. The exception of above-average weight and low glucose tolerance and its contribution to the development of NIDDM continues to be a major cause for concern.

The prevalence of risk factors contributing to HIV disease among Mexican Americans and non-Hispanic white drug injectors has recently been examined. Estrada showed that Mexican American drug injectors injected less frequently but disinfected their syringes less often and shared drug paraphernalia more often than Puerto Ricans or African Americans.[32] Condom use was almost nonexistent among this population. Additionally, a study examining HIV risk behaviors among Mexican-origin gay/bisexual males showed very high rates of unprotected sexual intercourse in combination with drug or alcohol use.[33]

MEXICAN AMERICAN WOMEN

> The menopause has brought on some problems that I'm faced with, that is the hot flashes, which are not pleasant. I have mild headaches when I don't take my hormonal dose. I get very bloated with water retention, which is very uncomfortable.... You also get very lethargic, as far as energy is concerned, unless you start taking your hormone supplements. (Gracie S., 46)

Some of the health issues affecting the lives of Mexican-origin women have already been mentioned. In this section we will highlight three additional issues: fertility patterns, prenatal care, and domestic violence.

The increase in the U.S. Mexican-origin population is primarily due to two factors: immigration and fertility rates. Among all Hispanic subgroups in the United States, Mexican American women have the highest **birth rates** and fertility rates.[34] Mexican American women have a birth rate of 28.7 per 1,000 compared to 15.7 per 1,000 for non-Hispanics. Further, the fertility rate for Mexican American women was 118.9 per 1,000 compared to 67.1 per 1,000 for non-Hispanics. Moreover, Mexican-origin women continue to have children well beyond what is typically referred to as the childbearing years (twenty to thirty-five years of age). These trends suggest a greater need for adequate maternal and child health services.

The age, educational level, and marital status of Mexican American women are important factors in determining the future welfare of both mothers and children. It is well known that Mexican Americans are generally younger than other Hispanic subgroups and non-Hispanics, and that their educational attainment levels are also lower. A study of fertility patterns and age structure found that 50 percent of all live births among Mexican American women occurred in the fifteen- to twenty-four-year age group in comparison to only 34 percent among non-Hispanic white women in the same age range.[35] Among mothers under twenty years of age, the percentage of unmarried mothers was very similar: 54 percent for Mexican American mothers compared to 55 percent for non-Hispanic white mothers. However, among mothers twenty years of age and older, 27 percent of Mexican American women compared to 12 percent of non-Hispanic white women were unmarried These trends suggest increased fertility as well as a potential increase in the "feminization of poverty," in that more Mexican American women become the single head of a household.

Appropriate prenatal care is very important to insure the health of both the developing fetus and the expectant mother. Early prenatal care can alert parents and physicians to the possibility of birth defects. Several factors contribute to the use of prenatal care—educational level, income, place of birth, and access to health care. Recent data show that Hispanic women tend to access and receive prenatal care at a lower rate than non-Hispanic whites. In their first trimester (the first three months of pregnancy) 87 percent of non-Hispanic white women received prenatal care compared to 72 percent of Hispanic women.[36] Clearly, more needs to be done to increase prenatal care among Hispanic women.

Domestic violence also affects the lives of many women. Exact figures are often not available due to the underreporting of domestic violence incidents. However, some studies have estimated that two to four million women annually are victims of domestic violence. Common types of injuries resulting from this violence include contusions, abrasions, and minor lacerations; fractures or sprains; and repeated chronic injuries. The stress of domestic violence may also cause psychiatric problems including depression, suicide attempts, feelings of isolation and an inability to cope, posttraumatic stress disorder, and alcohol or drug abuse. Obviously, the most detrimental potential result of domestic violence is the death of the abused person.

Exact domestic violence figures for Mexican-origin women are lacking. However, several domains contributing to domestic violence have been identified in the literature.[37] The **etiology** of domestic violence includes the male's need for power and control, lack of self-esteem, poor impulse control, dysfunctional family patterns, and rigid sex role expectations (**la sufrida**, *la mártir* [martyr], marianismo, machismo). Other sociocultural factors associated with domestic violence include acculturation level, underemployment, undereducation, economic stress, and the effects of the **Latino** male's experience of colonization, poverty, subordination, and exploitation.

Domestic violence is a cyclical process. Stress builds up in the male, who is unable to release it in appropriate ways, which then leads to aggression, then remorse. This cycle is often repeated indefinitely. More programs are needed that intervene and stop this cycle of violence.

AGRICULTURAL WORKERS   Mexican Americans are overrepresented in hazardous occupations. One of the most hazardous jobs that leads to increased morbidity and mortality is agricultural work. Such workers encounter five major health-related problems: accidents, pesticide-related illnesses, heat-related illnesses, musculoskeletal disorders, and communicable diseases.[38]

Machinery and farm vehicular accidents are the leading causes of death, injury, and traumatic amputation among agricultural workers. Nevertheless, specific information relating to Mexican-origin agricultural workers is sparse. What is known is that accidents are generally underreported. Most accidents happen during transportation to the fields or in the fields themselves. For example, it is not uncommon for agricultural workers to mistakenly cut off a finger while picking produce, given the monetary incentives to reap the harvest quickly. Agricultural workers who are unable to read English or Spanish not infrequently use machinery improperly, which could lead to devastating accidents.

Pesticide-related illnesses are a primary cause for concern since pesticide poisoning not only affects the person exposed, but also persons with whom the individual will come into contact, as well as the unborn. Pesticides are readily absorbed through the lungs, mouth, and skin. Exposure to pesticides may be direct or indirect. Direct exposure occurs through applying pesticides, entering a field where pesticides were recently sprayed, drift of pesticides from one field to an adjacent field, or contact with dry pesticide residue on produce. Indirect exposure may result from eating newly harvested fruit or vegetables without first washing them, eating or smoking with unwashed hands, and drinking or bathing in runoff from agricultural fields or barrels initially used for pesticides then converted into water containers. Pesticide poisoning has short- and long-term effects. Dermatitis, skin inflammation, and rashes are all common symptoms of direct pesticide exposure. Long-term exposure may lead to hematological (blood-system) cancers such as leukemia, Hodgkin's disease, and multiple myeloma. Effects may also occur in utero (in the womb), increasing the chance of damage to the developing fetus, which may result in birth defects.

Heat-related illnesses include heat stroke and heat exhaustion, primarily a result of severe dehydration and the lack of protective clothing. Again, due to the pressure to perform, agricultural workers may feel reluctant to take time out to drink sufficient water. Additionally, most of the work done in the fields is accomplished during the day, with full exposure to the sun. Without proper clothing or protection from the sun, workers can become overheated, resulting in heat stroke and heat exhaustion.

Musculoskeletal problems are a primary cause of physical impairment and activity limitation. Due to the type of work performed, many agricultural workers face long days of constant bending, stooping, kneeling, and heavy lifting. In addition, the now outlawed practice of using the short-handled hoe (mano del Diablo) contributed to the increase in lower-back problems and disability through constant stooping and bending.

There are at least three types of communicable diseases affecting agricultural workers: bacterial infections, parasitic infections, and viral infections. Among the bacterial infections, salmonellosis and shigellosis are probably the most common. These diseases are a direct result of poor sanitation in the fields or in dwellings. Parasitic diseases resulting from poor sanitary conditions, such as amebiasis, giardiasis, and *Ascaris lumbricoides*, also disproportionately affect agricultural workers and their families. Among the viral infections, hepatitis A, transmitted through poor sanitation and hygiene, can lead to liver problems and disability.

The Mexican American Morbidity and Mortality Paradox

The socioeconomic status of Mexican Americans is lower than that of non-Hispanic whites and comparable to that of African Americans. Yet researchers have noted what they term the morbidity-mortality paradox among Mexican Americans. With the exception of NIDDM, Mexican Americans generally have lower disease prevalence and disease mortality than non-Hispanics despite their disadvantaged socioeconomic backgrounds. Several hypotheses have been advanced to explain this paradox, but the two most common are the **salmon bias hypothesis** and the **healthy migrant hypothesis**.[39] The salmon bias hypothesis states that those Mexican Americans who may be near death return to Mexico because of a desire to die in their birthplace. Because these deaths are not accounted for in U.S. mortality statistics, these persons are said to be "statistically immortal," contributing to a lower apparent death rate among Mexican Americans. The healthy migrant hypothesis states that those Mexican Americans in the United States who emigrated from Mexico were generally healthier to begin with. Some researchers have also suggested that there are protective factors present in Mexican American culture that allow some degree of resistance to disease and death. Clearly, more research is needed to fully address the issues raised by this epidemiological paradox.

At the start of the twenty-first century several strategies need to be pursued to ameliorate the poor health status of Mexican Americans. These include improving health-care access through greater **financial access** and improving the quality of services. Better data are needed to assess health needs and outcomes so as to inform policymakers at all levels of government. More Hispanic health-care professionals are needed to assist in the development of culturally and **linguistically competent** health care programs for the Mexican-origin population. Both private and public partnerships are necessary to develop proven models to support health promotion and disease prevention within the Mexican-origin community. Clearly, such a shared vision is required if we are to close the gap in health care resources and improve the health of the Mexican-origin community in the United States.

Concluding Thoughts

This chapter has highlighted key health issues facing the Mexican-origin community as framed within the historical context of health and disease. In traditional indigenous Mesoamerican culture, a person's health depends on the forces of multiple souls in that individual, and the balance among these souls. The impact of the Spaniards on the Americas was profound and influenced or changed every aspect of the native cultures, including concepts of health, disease, and medicine. Combined legacies of the indigenous and Spanish cultures provide an important dimension for understanding health and disease in the Mexican-origin community. These early roots, coupled with the contemporary location of Mexican Americans within U.S. society, provide a framework that we can use to better understand the health status of this population. Understanding the cultural dimensions involved in health and medicine can help us in forming strategies to address the health problems faced by this community.

Effective strategies can be developed only with an understanding of the age- and gender-specific disease patterns faced by this population. For example, as a group, Mexican American children are seriously underimmunized against communicable diseases and infections. Other issues central to this age group, such as obesity and poor dental health, are related to poor diet and poverty. Mexican American adolescents are plagued with health problems such as NIDDM, and young Chicanas experience early sexual activity and teen pregnancy. Mexican-origin adults also encounter a higher incidence and prevalence of NIDDM. Complications resulting from late diagnosis and poor medical management of NIDDM are also more prevalent within the Mexican American community than the non-Hispanic white community. Other diseases affecting Mexican Americans include cancer, which is the second leading cause of death among Hispanics. A key strategy in lowering the incidence and prevalence of breast cancer and cervical cancer, the most common cancers among Mexican American women, is early detection and screening. Unfortunately, in practice the development of culturally and linguistically sensitive outreach and information programs to induce more Hispanic women to use preventive services is still in its infancy. Model programs must be developed and evaluated so that they may further enhance the health status of this growing community. Future research on Mexican American women's health should include the issues of underutilization of prenatal care and the extent of domestic violence.

Finally, **occupational location,** the type and economic sector of a person's employment, is a major influence on health-related injuries and diseases. This chapter focused on agricultural workers as an important subcategory of Mexican-origin people who are at greater health risk because of the work they perform. It is well established in the literature that farmworkers are more vulnerable to musculoskeletal diseases and pesticide poisoning as a result of their jobs. The unique occupational position of these workers requires additional sensitivity in screening and treatment of diseases. An important phenomenon that needs further study is the Mexican American morbidity and mortality paradox. Mexican Americans appear to have lower disease prevalence and disease mortality than non-Hispanics with similar socioeconomic characteristics, and it is urgent that we understand whether this is a result of cultural protective factors, physical characteristics, or simply inaccurate data.

■ Discussion Exercises

1. Discuss the origins of cultural beliefs about health and disease based on Aztec and European/Spanish concepts of medicine.

2. How does socioeconomic status affect the health status of Mexican Americans?

3. How do Mexican cultural beliefs and attitudes (machismo, marianismo, familismo, personalismo, etc.) influence the help-seeking behaviors and attitudes about health within the Mexican-origin population? What role does acculturation play in decisions regarding health?

4. Explain how the terms *incidence, prevalence, relative risk,* and *attributable risk* are useful in designing disease-prevention programs for the Mexican-origin community.

5. Discuss the three levels of disease prevention and give one example of each.

6. What factors affect the health status of Mexican American children? What are the major health issues facing this group? What issues emerge as these children progress through adolescence to adulthood?

7. Name some of the risk factors that can be modified to reduce the chance of diabetes, heart disease, and cancer.

8. How are Mexican American women affected by the issues of fertility patterns, prenatal care, and domestic violence? How do cultural beliefs and gender roles influence women's health decisions regarding these issues?

9. Discuss the reasons why Mexican-origin workers are disproportionately exposed to work-related environmental and safety hazards. What are some of the conditions that can result from this exposure?

10. What are some recommendations mentioned to improve the health status of Mexican Americans and Hispanics in general in the years to come? What would you recommend based on the information in this chapter?

■ Suggested Readings

Adams, D. L. *Health Issues for Women of Color: A Cultural Diversity Perspective.* Thousand Oaks, Calif.: Sage Publications, 1995.

Delgado, J. L. *Salud! A Latina's Guide to Total Health—Body Mind, and Spirit.* New York: HarperCollins, 1997.

Furino, A. *Health Policy and the Hispanic.* Boulder: Westview Press, 1992.

Hispanic Women and Cancer web site, The University of Arizona: http://w3.arizona.edu:180/masrc/hispanic_women/hispanic_women.htm.

Molina, C. W., and M. Aguirre-Molina, eds. *Latino Health in the U.S.: A Growing Challenge.* Washington, D.C.: American Public Health Association, 1994.

National Center for Health Statistics. *Health, United States, 1998* (with Socioeconomic Status and Health Chartbook). Hyattsville, Md.: U.S. Department of Health and Human Services, 1998.

Office of Minority Health Resource Center web site: http://www.omhrc.gov.

Plepys, C. *Health Status Indicators: Differentials by Race and Hispanic Origin.* Hyattsville, Md.: U.S. Dept. of Health and Human Services, 1995.

■ Notes

1. Mesoamerica refers to the area from central Mexico south and east through northern Central America.

2. B. R. Ortiz de Montellano, *Aztec Medicine, Health, and Nutrition* (New Brunswick, N.J.: Rutgers University Press, 1990).

3. I. Cuellar, B. Arnold, and R. Moldonado, "Acculturation Rating Scale for Mexican Americans–II: A Revision of the Original ARSMA Scale," *Hispanic Journal of Behavioral Sciences* 17, no. 3 (1995), pp. 275–304; see also C. Negy and D. J. Woods, "The Importance of Acculturation in Understanding Research with Hispanic Americans," *Hispanic Journal of Behavioral Sciences* 14, no. 2 (1992), pp. 224–47.

4. K. S. Markides, D. J. Lee, and L. A. Ray, "Acculturation and Hypertension in Mexican Americans," *Ethnicity and Disease* 3, no. 1 (1993), pp. 70–74; J. Sundquist and M. A. Winkleby, "Cardiovascular Risk Factors in Mexican American Adults: A Transcultural Analysis of NHANES III, 1988–1994," *American Journal of Public Health* 89, no. 5 (1999), pp. 723–30; J. M. Flack, H. Amaro, W. Jenkins, et al., "Epidemiology of Minority Health," *Health Psychology* 14, no. 7 (1995), pp. 592–600.

5. H. C. Triandas, *The Analysis of Subjective Culture* (New York: John Wiley, 1972).

6. R. Vargas and S. Martínez, *Razalogía: Community Learning for a New Society* (Oakland, Calif.: Razagente Associates, 1984).

7. S. J. Andrade and C. Doria-Ortiz, "Nuestro Bienestar: A Mexican-American Community-Based Definition of Health Promotion in the Southwestern United States," *Drugs: Education, Prevention, and Policy* 2, no. 2 (1995), 129–45.

8. P. Freire, *Pedagogy of the Oppressed* (New York: Continuum, 1995).

9. H. Rodríguez-Trias and A. B. Ramírez de Arellano, "The Health of Children and Youth," chap. 5 in *Latino Health in the United States: A Growing Challenge,* pp. 115–33 (Washington, D.C.: American Public Health Association, 1994).

10. National Center for Health Statistics, *Health, United States, 1998* (with Socioeconomic Status and Health Chartbook) (Hyattsville, Md.: National Center for Health Statistics, 1998).

11. U.S. Bureau of the Census, *Current Population Survey: March 1997* (Washington, D.C.: Government Printing Office, 1997).

12. HHANES is the most important and comprehensive survey of Hispanic health. It focuses on areas with high concentrations of specific Hispanic subpopulations. The Mexican-origin persons surveyed for the HHANES were living in five southwestern states. See A. de la Torre, R. Friis, H. Hunter, and L. García, "The Health Insurance Status of U.S. Latino Women: A Profile from the 1982–1984 HHANES," *American Journal of Public Health* 86, no. 4 (April 1996), pp. 533–37.

13. National Center for Health Statistics, *Health, United States, 1998.*

14. P. J. Gergen, T. Ezzati, and H. Russell, "DTP Immunization Status and Tetanus Antitoxin Status of Mexican American Children Ages Six Months through Eleven Years," *American Journal of Public Health* 78 (1988), pp. 1446–50.

15. National Center for Health Statistics, *Health, United States, 1998.*

16. A. I. Ismail and S. M. Szpunar, "The Prevalence of Total Tooth Loss, Dental Caries, and Periodontal Disease among Mexican Americans, Cuban Americans, and Puerto Ricans: Findings from HHANES 1982–1984," *American Journal of Public Health* 80, suppl. (1990), pp. 66–70.

17. H. S. Glaser and K. L. Jones, "Non-insulin Dependent Diabetes Mellitus in Mexican American Children," *Western Journal of Medicine* 168, no. 1 (1998), pp. 11–16.

18. D. Neufeld, Y.D.I. Chen, et al., "Early Presentation of Type 2 Diabetes in Mexican American Youth," *Diabetes Care* 21 (1998), pp. 80–86.

19. D. De Anda, R. M. Becerra, and P. Fielder, "Sexuality, Pregnancy, and Motherhood among Mexican American Adolescents," *Journal of Adolescent Research* 3 (1988), pp. 403–11; see also W. D. Mosher, and J. W. McNally, "Contraceptive Use at First Premarital Intercourse: United States, 1965–1988," *Family Planning Perspectives I* 23 (1991), pp. 108–16.

20. National Center for Health Statistics, *Deaths of Hispanic Origin, Vital and Health Statistics* ser. 20, no. 18 (1990).

21. Centers for Disease Control and Prevention, *The Health of America's Youth: Current Trends in Health Status and Health Services* (Atlanta, Ga.: Centers for Disease Control and Prevention, 1991).

22. Centers for Disease Control and Prevention, "Self-Reported Prevalence of Diabetes among Hispanics—United States, 1994–1997," *Mortality and Morbidity Weekly Report* (January 15, 1999).

23. J. C. Bolen, L. Rhodes, E. E. Powell-Griner, S. D. Bland, and D. Holtzman, "State-Specific Prevalence of Selected Health Behaviors, by Race and Ethnicity—Behavioral Risk Factor Surveillance System, 1997." *Morbidity and Mortality Weekly Report* 49 (SS02) (March 24, 2000), 1–60.

24. M. Harris, D. E. Goldstein, K. M. Flegal, et al., "Prevalence of Diabetes, Impaired Fasting Glucose, and Impaired Glucose Tolerance in U.S. Adults: The Third National Health and Nutrition Examination Survey, 1988–1994," *Diabetes Care* 21 (1998), pp. 518–24.

25. S. M. Haffner, M. P. Stern, F. D. Hazuda, et al., "Role of Obesity and Fat Distribution in Non-insulin Dependent Diabetes Mellitus in Mexican Americans and Non-Hispanic Whites," *Diabetes Care* 9 (1986), pp. 153–61; E. J. Boyko et al., "Higher Insulin and C-peptide Concentrations in Hispanic Populations at High Risk for NIDDM: San Luis Valley Diabetes Study," *Diabetes* 40 (1991), pp. 509–15.

26. Due to data limitations, some statistics cited in this chapter include all Hispanics. Since Mexican-origin persons are the largest subpopulation of Hispanics, useful inferences can be made from these data.

27. UPI, "Study: Risk of Coronary Disease Higher in Hispanics," UPI Science Report (November 8, 1998).

28. National Institutes of Health, "Study First to Show Mexican Americans Hospitalized More Often for Heart Attack than Non-Hispanic Whites." NIH Publication #97-4517, 1997.

29. Centers for Disease Control and Prevention, National Center for Health Statistics, Division of Health Interview Statistics, *Data from the National Health Interview Survey* (Atlanta, Ga.: Centers for Disease Control and Prevention, 1995).

30. T. Díaz, J. W. Buehler, K. G. Castro, and J. W. Ward, "AIDS Trends among Hispanics in the United States," *American Journal of Public Health* 83 (1993), pp. 504–9.

31. A. L. Estrada, "Drug Use and HIV Risks among African American, Mexican American, and Puerto Rican Drug Injectors," *Journal of Psychoactive Drugs* 30, no. 3 (1998), pp. 247–53.

32. Ibid.

33. A. L. Estrada, "HIV Risk Behaviors among Gay Latinos Residing in the U.S.–Mexico Border Area." Paper presented to the 120th Annual Meeting of the American Public Health Association, Washington, D.C., April 1992.

34. A. Giachello, "Maternal/Perinatal Health," chap. 6 in *Latino Health in the United States: A Growing Challenge,* eds. C. W. Molina and M. Aguirre-Molina (Washington, D.C.: American Public Health Association, 1994).

35. Ibid.

36. "Eliminating Racial and Ethnic Disparities in Health" (Washington, D.C.: Grant Makers in Health, September 1998).

37. M. M. Zambrana, *Mejor Sola que Mal Acompañada: For the Latina in an Abusive Relationship* (Seattle: The Seal Press, 1985).

38. G. Friedman-Jiménez and J. S. Ortiz, "Occupational Health," chap. 12 in *Latino Health in the United States: A Growing Challenge,* eds. C. W. Molina and M. Aguirre-Molina (Washington, D.C.: American Public Health Association, 1994).

39. A. F. Abraido-Lanza, B. P. Dohrenwend, D. S. Ng-Mak, and J. B. Turner, "The Latino Mortality Paradox: A Test of the 'Salmon Bias' and Healthy Migrant Hypotheses," *American Journal of Public Health* 89 (1999), pp. 1543–48.

3

"One starts with marijuana . . ."

UNDERSTANDING SUBSTANCE
ABUSE AND AIDS

The **co-occurrence** of substance use, violence, and HIV/AIDS risk behaviors poses serious problems for the **Mexican American** community. In this chapter we will examine several topics: (1) the **epidemiology** (patterns) of substance use among Mexican American adolescents and
adults; (2) the available evidence on the cause of substance use; (3) the co-
occurrence of substance abuse with violence and HIV/AIDS; and (4) issues
related to prevention of substance abuse among youth and adolescents.

The twin **epidemics** of substance abuse and human immunodeficiency
virus/acquired immunodeficiency syndrome (HIV/AIDS) are cause for particular concern among **Hispanics**.[1] According to the Centers for Disease
Control and Prevention (CDC), in 1998 injection drug use accounted for 36
percent of AIDS cases among Hispanic male adults and adolescents, 41
percent of AIDS cases among Hispanic female adults and adolescents, and
was indirectly responsible for 92 percent of Hispanic pediatric AIDS cases.[2]
However, in order to address substance abuse, violence, and HIV/AIDS prevention for Hispanics, it becomes very important to differentiate **epidemiological patterns** associated with increased risk among the various
Hispanic subgroups (Puerto Rican, Cuban, Central or South American,
Mexican American). These Hispanic subgroups may exhibit different
drug use patterns, and understanding such differences can maximize the
chances for successful substance abuse treatment and HIV/AIDS prevention
programs.

Few national databases on substance abuse or HIV/AIDS differentiate
among the major Hispanic subgroups. This lack of differentiation has
resulted in the spread of many substance abuse and HIV/AIDS prevention
strategies that are too generic to be meaningful. We must ask ourselves
whether it continues to make sense to implement prevention models that
do not incorporate key cultural elements related to behavioral change of
the minority groups with whom we work. Do cultural prevention models

have greater impact on reducing substance abuse, violence, or HIV/AIDS than do generic models? Could prevention resources be better used if the **epidemiological profiles** of Hispanic subgroups are matched to **primary, secondary,** and **tertiary prevention** efforts? Are cultural models of prevention more cost-effective than generic models? These questions, and others, need to be addressed if we wish to be truly responsive to the heartfelt needs of people living with and dying from the adverse health consequences of drug use.

 ## Prevalence of Drug Use among Mexican American Adolescents and Adults

> Once one is involved in drugs, bad company follows, problems, jail, etc., etc., fights, violence. This is what drugs bring into one's life and nothing else. That is what I believe because I have gone through it so much, and I would not want today's youth to fall into the clutches of vice. It would make me very happy that they would listen to me and that they would attend to my words.
> (Enrique A., 30)

Since large national databases usually do not differentiate among Hispanic subgroups, the data available can only provide a picture of substance abuse trends among Hispanics in general. The epidemiology of substance abuse among Hispanic adolescents can be assessed through existing databases and research findings. Sources such as the Youth Risk Behavior Survey,[3] the Monitoring the Future Study,[4] the National Household Survey on Drug Abuse,[5] and findings from the Hispanic Health and Nutrition Examination Survey[6] (HHANES) are particularly appropriate to examine.

Hispanic Adolescents

> [W]hen I was at Edison Elementary School . . . my friends were already using drugs. I chose it [marijuana] because it was available. From there [I] tried pills, cocaine, and well, in school, as a youth, one does not know how to say no. One starts with marijuana, then cocaine followed by heroin, ending with more dangerous substances. (Enrique A., 30)

Among both males and females twelve to fifteen years of age, lifetime use of (that is, whether one has ever used) alcohol, marijuana, and cocaine was higher for Hispanic youth than for other racial and ethnic groups. For youth sixteen years of age or older, Hispanic males and females had higher rates than African Americans but lower rates than **non-Hispanic** whites for lifetime use of alcohol; however, they had higher lifetime **prevalence** rates for marijuana, cocaine, and crack cocaine use than non-Hispanic whites, and in some instances higher rates than African Americans of the same age and gender.[7] These trends suggest that drug use in Hispanic communities begins early and continues well into the late teen years at higher rates than for African Americans and non-Hispanic whites.

Hispanic Adults

> I believe that once you are an alcoholic or an addict, you are always an alcoholic or an addict, and you have to be careful of backsliding. (Danny F., 36)

In 1991, the National Institute on Drug Abuse (NIDA) National Household Survey examined adult usage of illegal drugs.[8] The survey noted several trends:

■ About one-third of Hispanics had used an illegal drug at least once during their life, and just less than 7 percent reported using an illegal drug in the past month.

■ The top two illegal drugs used were marijuana (27 percent) and cocaine (11 percent).

■ The rate of use of other illegal drugs was less than 7 percent.

These data suggest that the primary drug of choice for Hispanic adults is marijuana, with the use of other illegal drugs at much lower rates. Overall, it would appear that among Hispanic adults, illegal drug use is lower than for non-Hispanic whites.

Although information specific to the various Hispanic subgroups is not easily attainable, one study sheds light on key differences and patterns among the major Hispanic subgroups. Conducted in 1982–1984, HHANES was an attempt to determine the prevalence of the use of marijuana, cocaine, inhalants, and sedatives among Mexican Americans, Puerto Ricans, and Cuban Americans ages twelve to forty-four.[9]

Among Mexican Americans, those who were younger, male, English speakers, native-born, and with higher educational levels had higher marijuana use rates. Subgroup differences were observed with relation to cocaine use as well, with individuals ages eighteen to thirty-four being two to four times more likely than those of other age groups ever to have used cocaine. More men reported use than women; more English speakers than Spanish speakers; more well educated than less educated; and more native-born than **foreign-born**. The sociodemographic subgroups that had higher rates of reported inhalant use were younger, male, and native-born. The subgroups most likely to use sedatives were older age groups, males, English speakers, and those born in the United States. Unfortunately, HHANES did not include data on heroin use and crack cocaine use, partially because crack had not yet emerged as a drug of choice during the data-collection phase of HHANES.

These findings suggest several trends. First, an individual's level of **acculturation** is highly correlated with drug use; more acculturated Hispanics show higher rates of use than less acculturated Hispanics. Second, more Mexican American males than females use legal and illegal drugs. Third, use of several different types of drugs—in particular marijuana, inhalants, and cocaine—is higher among Mexican American adolescents than non-Hispanic white adolescents.

Injection Drug Use among Mexican Americans

The "hidden" nature of the drug-injecting population makes accurate estimates difficult; however, Ginzburg estimated that there were at least 350,000 heroin injectors in the United States.[10] Because drug injectors may inject several drugs, not just heroin, the number of injectors of any drug could be three to four times the number of heroin users. Hispanics and other minority groups are probably overrepresented in this group, yet surprisingly little is known about the prevalence of injection drug use and associated risks among Hispanics in general and Mexican Americans in particular. Data collected as part of NIDA's household survey reported only a 2.2 percent prevalence rate for any use of needles among Mexican Americans.[11]

◼ Causal Factors in Substance Use

Several causal factors are reported in the substance abuse literature. These factors fall into three broad areas: social context, individual/interpersonal factors, and acculturation.

Social Context and the Initiation of Substance Use

Factors considered in the area of social context include laws and norms favorable to substance use, availability of legal and illegal drugs, low socioeconomic status, unemployment, crime, and poverty levels in particular neighborhoods.

Laws and social or cultural norms that are favorable toward drug use are considered to be **modifiable risk factors**; that is, they are amenable to change. Even though laws related to age of purchase for tobacco and alcohol exist in many states, youth can still obtain these substances relatively easily through falsified identification or by having older individuals purchase these products for them. Norms favoring the use of certain substances are also prevalent. For example, it is not uncommon for parents to purchase alcohol for their children to drink at their own parties with parental supervision. This act sends a message that alcohol consumption is okay if conducted under parental supervision. Norms among youth also tend to encourage consumption of both alcohol and illegal drugs.

> I used street drugs. . . . I think smoking weed and drinking a little bit of beer was like a daily thing. (Danny F., 36)

Availability of both legal and illegal drugs is another important factor contributing to use. Many studies have shown that when drugs are easily available, use tends to increase.[12] Perceived availability of drugs is correlated with age and grade level of students, with older students in higher grades having higher rates of use and greater perceived availability.

Typically, those who live at or below the **federal poverty level** also live in neighborhoods where there is a high prevalence of crime, including drug dealing and drug use. Since Mexican Americans tend to reside in neighborhoods *(barrios)* where these factors coexist, it is not surprising that consumption of both legal and illegal drugs tends to be higher.

Individual and Interpersonal Factors in the Initiation of Substance Use

> A lot of my friends started using and I never wanted to use. Little by little they came up . . . [to me] telling me that they started getting high. One of the major things is that I always wanted to identify with something and ever since I was nine years old, I started getting lost, like where's my place. (Danny F., 36)

Factors related to drug use include poor family management, association with drug-using peers, early onset of drug use, and antisocial behavior. Family management issues include lack of clear expectations for behavior, lack of monitoring, lack of caring, and inconsistent or excessively severe discipline. These are significantly correlated with initiation and maintenance of substance use. For example, a study of in-school youth in the Arizona-Sonora border area found that more than one-third of tenth graders were allowed to stay out past 10:00 P.M. during school nights, and more than 50 percent were allowed to stay out past midnight on weekends.[13] Such lack of parental monitoring can easily lead to substance use among youth.

Other studies have shown that association with drug-using peers is highly correlated with substance use, and that peer pressure to use both legal and illegal drugs is not uncommon. As noted previously, there has been an increase in the use and social acceptability of a number of drugs. This trend is accompanied by a similar increase in reported use of substances among friends. This relationship reflects several different patterns: a person with friends who use a drug will be more likely to try that drug, a person who is already using a drug will be more likely to introduce friends to the experience, and users are more likely to establish friendships with other users.[14] Peer approval of drug use is also correlated with initiation and maintenance. The study of in-school youth in the Arizona-Sonora border region found that 23 percent of tenth graders' friends would approve of alcohol use, and 15 percent would approve of marijuana use.[15]

Early onset of substance use is also associated with maintenance of substance use behaviors. The National Household Survey on Drug Abuse reported age of first use of cigarettes, alcohol, and marijuana for youth ages twelve to seventeen years.[16] Between 1990 and 1996, Hispanic youth initiated cigarette smoking on average at twelve years of age compared to eleven years of age for African American and non-Hispanic white youth. Hispanic youth initiated alcohol use at a slightly older age than non-Hispanic whites but a younger age than African Americans. For marijuana use, Hispanic, non-Hispanic white, and African American youth initiated use at comparable ages, approximately fourteen years of age.

Antisocial behavior is also highly correlated with substance use, as shown in table 3.1. Although the percentages of antisocial behavior with marijuana use are high, the percentage increases with cocaine use in the past thirty days.[17] Among youths who had not used drugs within the past

Table 3.1 Correlation of Antisocial Behavior with Drug Use among Adolescents

DRUG USED IN PAST 30 DAYS	NON-HISPANIC WHITE		HISPANIC	
	INVOLVED IN FIGHT[1] (%)	CARRIED WEAPON[1] (%)	INVOLVED IN FIGHT[1] (%)	CARRIED WEAPON[1] (%)
MARIJUANA	51	32	68	46
COCAINE	83	70	68	57
NO DRUG USE	30	14	39	16

1. In the past year.

Source: *Youth Risk Behavior Survey* (Atlanta, Ga.: Centers for Disease Control and Prevention, 1995).

month, antisocial behavior was more frequently reported by Hispanic than non-Hispanic white respondents.

Cultural Factors in the Initiation of Substance Use

When you are drugged up you look for fights at school, you make graffiti, you fight with other members of the gang. It would make us so mad when they would call us "wetbacks." That is why we joined that gang, because we were wetbacks, and as time went by, more wetbacks joined the gang. Being in the company of five or ten friends, all under the influence of drugs, we would beat people to unconsciousness with sticks or whatever you want to call it! (Enrique A., 30)

Some research has shown that acculturation level is correlated with both legal and illegal drug use. Felix-Ortiz and Newcomb suggest that research must extend the concept of acculturation to be more inclusive of cultural identity.[18] For them, cultural identity more accurately represents the process that occurs as part of personality formation among Hispanic adolescents. They suggest several ways in which cultural identity can affect drug use. It may increase risk for persons who strongly identify as Mexican American because their values and behavior conflict with those of the dominant culture. Conversely, cultural identity may be protective, in that persons who strongly identify with Mexican American culture may be at reduced risk because Mexican American values and behavior do not support use of drugs. Similarly, bicultural identity may be risk-increasing due to the stress of negotiating two cultures (**acculturative stress**); or, it may be protective due to the adaptive integration of persons who have the skills to negotiate both cultures.[19]

To date, research findings linking acculturation, cultural identity, or acculturative stress to substance use among Hispanics has been ambiguous at best. Clearly, a more extensive examination is needed of the multiple and complex interactions among culture, discrimination and prejudice, and socioeconomic status in relation to substance use.

 ## The Co-occurrence of Violence and Substance Use among Mexican American Adolescents

> My mother . . . left to go take care of her mom when I was fourteen . . . I never wanted to be in a gang, and I never wanted to use drugs or alcohol. . . . There was substance abuse in my house. There was violence, and it became a hopeless place and a lot of my friends started using and I never wanted to use. (Danny F., 36)

Several studies on violence and substance use have found a high correlation between the two, yet a causal relationship is difficult to establish without **longitudinal data** that follow a group of people over many years. Otherwise, it is difficult to disentangle which came first, drug use or violence. Some research has indicated that the interrelationship between drug use and violence is complex, depending in part on the drug consumed, the personality of the person consuming the drug, and the context in which the two coexist. Clearly, several factors are involved in this relationship; for example, low self-esteem, poor academic performance, and delinquency. Poor academic performance is higher among Hispanic than other youth. Moreover, Chávez, Edwards, and Oetting found that school dropouts and students with poor academic achievement were more likely to be both perpetrators and victims of violence.[20] Among Mexican American youth in the study, those who were dropouts had higher rates of being beaten by parents or peers, stabbed, or shot than those Mexican American students in good or even poor academic standing.

Adverse Health Consequences of Drug Use

Drug use has serious health consequences, including HIV/AIDS and related risk behaviors, drug-related emergency room episodes, and drug related deaths.

HIV/AIDS and Related Behaviors

As mentioned previously, among Hispanic men, injection drug use accounts for 36 percent of reported AIDS cases, and among Hispanic women it accounts for 41 percent of AIDS cases.[21] In the Southwest, where the vast majority of Hispanics are of Mexican origin, AIDS rates attributed to injection drug use range from a high of 13.3 percent in Arizona to a low of 6.9 percent in California.[22]

Although examining **incidence** and prevalence rates is important, attention must also focus on the **behavioral epidemiology** of HIV risk among Mexican American injection drug users (IDUs). This focus must include many injection and sexual risk behaviors if we are to fully understand activities conducive to HIV transmission and develop appropriate strategies to reduce these risks. Several studies have characterized risk behaviors associated with HIV transmission among IDUs.[23] Briefly, these behaviors include the frequency of drug injection, the frequency and proportion of injection with used needles, the number of needle/syringe-sharing partners, injection with specific drugs such as heroin, cocaine, and heroin mixtures (**speedballs**), and indirect sharing of drug-injection equipment such as **cookers, cotton,** and the **rinse water.**

Unfortunately, few studies focus on Mexican-origin Hispanics, and fewer still focus on the prevalence of HIV risk behaviors in the U.S.–Mexico border area or differences in risk behaviors among specific Hispanic subgroups. However, some existing studies have significant implications for HIV risk reduction on the border.

Estrada and colleagues reported on the prevalence of HIV risk behaviors in the Southwest in a study comparing border-area Hispanics (those residing in Arizona, California, and Texas), with non-border-area Hispanics, non-Hispanic whites, and African Americans.[24] The findings indicated that border-area Hispanics were most likely to share needles with two or more persons (74 percent), with non-Hispanic whites next most likely (65 percent), followed by African Americans (59 percent) then non-border-area Hispanics (58 percent). Border-area Hispanics were less likely than African Americans and non-border-area Hispanics always to use a clean needle. Moreover, they were less likely to use bleach (which kills the HIV virus) as a disinfectant than the other three groups.

In a recent study examining HIV needle risk behaviors in a national sample of drug injectors (collected as part of the NIDA Cooperative Agreement Program), there was a trend for Mexican Americans to share needles and other drug paraphernalia within their drug-using social networks. Also, Mexican American IDUs did not use bleach very often to disinfect their needles.[25]

Clearly, given the frequent sharing of injection equipment with others in the drug-using social network, the high frequency of injection, and the general lack of adequate disinfection among Mexican American IDUs, this group is sitting on a time bomb. It is indeed fortunate that the HIV **seroprevalence** is low (on average about 3 to 5 percent) among Mexican American drug injectors in the Southwest. The prevalence of hepatitis B and C is very high among injection drug users, however. These studies suggest that HIV/AIDS risk-reduction programs should specifically target the needle-using social network of Mexican American injectors.

Among IDUs, risk of HIV transmission via sex remains particularly high.[26] Behaviors to be targeted in order to reduce HIV risk include frequency of condom use; exchanging sex for money, drugs, or both; and the number of sexual partners who are IDUs. With respect to exchanging sex for money and/or drugs, Mexican American IDUs reported exchanging sex for money or drugs an average of less than once in the last thirty days. However, condom use was found to be almost nonexistent. Additionally, other research with Mexican American IDUs has found that few make the connection between risky needle practices and the risk of HIV transmission to a non-IDU partner through unprotected sex. This connection needs to be made explicit for both the IDU and his or her sexual partner. Moreover, some injection methods, namely **backloading** and **frontloading**, involve sharing syringes rather than needles. Syringe sharing usually occurs with a common or pooled purchase of the injected drug. Because the syringe may become contaminated with blood, syringe sharing is another possible means of HIV transmission. Risk behaviors among Mexican American IDUs are unlikely to change if prevention efforts focus on needle sharing while ignoring syringe sharing and the reasons for doing so, and focus on condom use without making an explicit connection between needle risk and sexual risk.

> The sexual power is also seen in some men who are machistas, that because they are married or have a common-law wife or have a girlfriend, they can also engage in having sex with other men as long as they are not identified as being homosexual, as being a gay

individual . . . compounding that with alcohol or any other drug use, the power increases. (Ernie P., 40)

Men who have sex with men and inject drugs pose threats for HIV transmission both among themselves and to others. However, few studies have examined injection drug use among gay men and fewer still have examined this issue among Mexican Americans. Estrada and colleagues focused on HIV risk behaviors among straight and gay/bisexual drug injectors. They found the frequency of injection to be significantly higher among straight than among gay/bisexual IDUS.[27] On the other hand, gay/bisexual IDUS had significantly higher prevalence rates of always **renting needles**; sharing the cooker, cotton, or rinse water; and borrowing used needles. Further, gay/bisexual IDUS had significantly higher rates than straight IDUS of always sharing needles with others in their social networks. Moreover, straight IDUS were more than twice as likely as gay/bisexual IDUS always to clean their needles with bleach.

HISPANIC YOUTH AND ADOLESCENTS Several studies have shown that Hispanic adolescents are among the least informed about HIV/AIDS of all ethnic groups, and they generally have more misconceptions about HIV transmission than others.[28] Most youth do not perceive themselves to be at risk for HIV infection,[29] nor do they usually change their behaviors as a consequence of HIV information.[30]

Sexuality and sexual knowledge among Hispanic youth are not well understood, but a few studies have been completed. Davis and Harris examined knowledge of sex-related words and found that Hispanic students were less likely than non-Hispanic whites to know what a condom was.[31] These authors also reported that Hispanic adolescents receive less sexual information from their parents than non-Hispanic white students do. Further, Moore and Erickson found Hispanic students to have less factual knowledge about sexuality, particularly birth control, than African Americans or non-Hispanic whites.[32] However, these authors found no significant differences between Hispanics and other ethnic groups in sexual behavior such as frequency of intercourse, contraception use, pregnancy history, talking about birth control and sexually transmitted diseases with partners, and age of first sexual intercourse.

In terms of HIV/AIDS education strategies, most adolescents prefer peer-based strategies that are innovative and that do not "just talk about the same old thing." Most adolescents say they would like an HIV-positive person to talk to them about AIDS, to show what the disease does to the body. It is difficult for most youth to identify readily with a disease like AIDS that shows no symptoms for a period of many years. Thus, HIV/AIDS prevention among Mexican American youth must be threefold: (1) increasing awareness of sexual behaviors that can lead to HIV/AIDS infection, (2) increasing the understanding that drug use is an HIV risk factor, and (3) reducing HIV risk behaviors currently practiced.

HISPANIC WOMEN In general, female IDUs who are in a relationship are likely to be with a man who is also an IDU; conversely, the majority of male IDUs are in primary relationships with women who do not use drugs.[33] Women IDUs are also reported to have more medical problems than their male counterparts, including poor nutrition, repeated infections, and sexually transmitted diseases. They also may experience more stress because of responsibility for children, lack of support from family, lack of financial resources, anxiety, and low self-esteem.[34] These women may also turn to prostitution as a means of financial support. Noninjecting women who are in relationships with male IDUs are confronted with similar economic and emotional issues. A major difference, however, is that women who do not inject drugs may not perceive themselves as being at risk, not realizing that a sexual relationship with an IDU may put them and their future offspring in danger.[35] Failure to recognize such risks is exacerbated in many relationships where the male hides his drug use from his spouse or significant other.[36]

There are only a small number of promising interventions that target female sexual partners of IDUs. One is the WHEEL project (Women Helping to Empower and Enhance Lives), sponsored by NIDA. This intervention focuses on educating such women so that they will become empowered to take responsibility for their own health and safety. Strategies include educating them about their HIV transmission risks, increasing their awareness and confronting denial, training them in skills necessary for negotiating and practicing safer sex, counseling them in methods of negotiating safer sex practices with their partner(s), and educating them in how to obtain needed resources from community service agencies and advocacy groups.

Drug-Related Emergency Room Episodes

Drug-related hospital emergency room episodes provide an important measure of the health risks associated with drug use. Records of these visits

Table 3.2 Hispanic Drug-Related Illnesses Based on Emergency Room Admissions and Medical Examiner Data

DRUG	DRUG-RELATED ADMISSIONS (%)	INCREASE IN ADMISSIONS, 1988–1994 (%)
Alcohol in combination with		
drugs	28.3	—
Cocaine	26.5	22
Heroin/morphine	18.9	44
Acetaminophen	8.4	—
Marijuana/hashish	6.2	88

Source: Substance Abuse and Mental Health Services Administration (SAMHSA), *Data from the Drug Abuse Warning Network* (DAWN), 1994 data file (Rockville, Md.: SAMHSA, 1994).

indicate increases or decreases in the incidence of problems associated with a particular drug or drug combination. The primary source of data on drug-related emergency room visits is the Drug Abuse Warning Network (DAWN), a large-scale, ongoing data collection system that monitors the adverse consequences of drug abuse as reported by selected hospital emergency rooms and medical examiner's offices in the nation.[37] As shown in table 3.2, among Hispanics the five drugs most frequently mentioned were alcohol in combination with other drugs, cocaine, heroin/morphine, acetaminophen, and marijuana/hashish.

Among Hispanics there was a 30 percent overall increase in drug-related emergency room visits from 1988 to 1994. Table 3.3 shows the percentage of emergency room admissions of male and female Hispanics due to drug-related causes. These emergency room admissions are further broken down into the percentage of drug users who had used a single drug versus a combination of drugs.

Drug-Related Deaths

DAWN defines a drug-related death as any death in which drug use is a contributory factor but not necessarily the sole cause; consequently, drug use need not be the direct cause of death. As a result some medical examiners may use circumstantial evidence in reporting drug-related deaths whereas others may report only deaths confirmed through toxicological analysis. Thus, the information in table 3.4 should be viewed with these limitations in mind. Overall, 79 percent of drug-related deaths among Hispanics were deemed accidental; that is, due to an unintentional drug

Table 3.3 Hispanic Drug-Related Emergency Room Admissions (as Percentage of All Admissions)

REASON FOR ADMISSION	MALES (%)	FEMALES (%)
All drug-related incidents	32.5	44.4
Single-drug episode	52.6	59.4
Multi-drug episode	47.4	40.6

Source: SAMHSA, Data from DAWN, 1994 data file (Rockville, Md.: SAMHSA, 1994).

Table 3.4 Drug-Related Deaths among Hispanics

DRUG	DEATHS ATTRIBUTED TO DRUG (% OF ALL DRUG-RELATED DEATHS)[1]
Heroin/morphine	55.9
Cocaine	55.1
Alcohol in combination with drugs	48.3
Codeine	12.9
Marijuana/hashish	7.6

1. Includes both deaths directly caused by drug use and deaths in which drug use was a contributory factor. Percentages total more than 100 because of cases involving use of multiple drugs.

Source: SAMHSA, Data from DAWN, 1994 data file (Rockville, Md.: SAMHSA, 1994).

overdose. Only 9.9 percent of Hispanic drug-related deaths were the result of suicide.

Other Adverse Health Effects of Substance Abuse

Beyond HIV/AIDS, drug overdoses, and drug-related deaths, there are several other adverse consequences of substance abuse. Particularly significant are the **morbidity** and **mortality** related to tobacco and alcohol consumption. Hispanics, especially Mexican Americans, have higher prevalence rates of cirrhosis of the liver and chronic liver disease than do non-Hispanic whites. Additionally, the incidence of lung cancer and cardiovascular disease among Hispanics is directly linked to the chronic use of tobacco products and alcohol. The use of alcohol and other drugs also contributes to injuries and motor vehicle accidents, which are the fourth leading cause of mortality among twenty-four- to forty-four-year-old Hispanics. Further, the use of alcohol, tobacco, and other drugs is associated with depression, antisocial personality, and organic brain damage. Needle sharing and lack of needle hygiene among IDUs lead to increased prevalence and incidence of hepatitis B and hepatitis C. Clearly, the association of substance use with other forms of morbidity and mortality will continue if steps are not taken to prevent substance use or intervene with those who are presently using substances.

 ## Prevention Issues among Hispanic Youth and Adolescents

I recommend that today's young people . . . take education seriously so they would have less problems finding good jobs and a good place [healthy community] to live in. (Enrique A., 30)

We have seen that substance use among youth and adults involves a number of different and co-occurring factors. Taken together, these factors form the "web of causation" comprised of individual characteristics, characteristics of the family, peer group influences, and the general social environment. Despite the specific risk factors contributing to adolescent substance abuse, there are also resiliency and protective factors that can be marshaled to delay or prevent the initiation of substance use. These positive factors are not conceptualized simply as the opposite of risk factors. Rather, they interact with risk factors to mitigate, or lessen, their effect. The idea of identifying protective processes or specifying particular interactions among **variables** that produce resilience has direct relevance for risk-focused drug abuse prevention. Moreover, due to the interactive and often synergistic nature of many risk factors, prevention strategies should focus on simultaneously reducing multiple risks and enhancing multiple protective factors. Research has demonstrated that as protective factors increase, substance abuse decreases. Conversely, as risk factors increase, so does substance use.[38]

Four attributes have been consistently identified as describing resilient youth:

■ *social competence,* which includes the qualities of responsiveness, flexibility, empathy and caring, communication skills, sense of humor, and prosocial behavior

■ *problem solving,* which includes skills such as abstract, reflective, and flexible thinking and identifying multiple solutions for both cognitive and social problems

■ *autonomy,* or a sense of one's own identity and the ability to act independently and exert some control over one's environment

■ *a sense of purpose/future,* which includes healthy expectancies for the future, goal-directedness, success orientation, achievement motivation, educational aspirations, persistence, hopefulness, belief in a bright future, and a sense of coherence

Other factors critical to the positive development of youth are a caring, supportive family environment in which adults have high and clear expectations and provide children with opportunities to participate meaningfully in the family. Four general substance abuse prevention strategies have been used with adolescents: providing knowledge and information, affective education (empathy and interpersonal skills), social resistance skills training (for example, how to refuse drugs while maintaining friendships), and personal and social skills training.[39]

Approaches that provide information typically focus on the negative impact of substance use on academic performance, interpersonal relations, and social functioning. Additionally, these approaches provide information on patterns of drug use and the pharmacology of drugs. As Botvin notes, these approaches assume that given accurate information, people will make a rational decision on whether or not to use drugs.[40] In fact, however, information-based approaches have shown little effectiveness in changing behavior.

Affective education approaches emphasize personal and social development of youth. Psychosocial factors in the **etiology** of substance use are a prime focus in this approach—for example, that substance abuse tends to be correlated with low self-esteem and poor social skills. The theory is that intervening to improve social skills and self-esteem, without focusing directly on drugs, will make youth less vulnerable to substance use. Again, however, research studies have failed to demonstrate the effectiveness of this approach in reducing drug use.

Social resistance skills training appears to be a promising approach. This approach attempts to **psychologically inoculate** youth by giving them social skills to resist peer pressure to use drugs. Personal and social skills training emphasize the teaching of generic personal self-management skills and social skills. Examples include decision-making and problem-solving skills; cognitive skills for resisting peer, family, and media influences; skills for enhancing self-esteem; and adaptive coping responses, among others. This approach differs from the others in that it addresses a wide range of skills relevant to the youths' social environment. It appears to be a promising approach to reducing substance use among adolescents.

◼ Concluding Thoughts

Substance abuse is a significant problem facing the Mexican-origin community. An individual's level of acculturation is highly correlated with drug use: more acculturated Hispanics tend to have higher rates of use of legal and illegal substances than do less acculturated Hispanics. More Mexican American males than females use legal and illegal drugs. Use of marijuana, inhalants, and heroin is greater among Mexican American adolescents than non-Hispanic white adolescents. IDUS are a small but important group within the Hispanic population because Hispanics are overrepresented in this segment of drug users.

Some studies have linked antisocial behavior to substance abuse, although it is unclear which comes first. What is clear are the health consequences of drug use. For example, among Hispanic men, IDUS account for more than one-third of all reported AIDS cases; among Hispanic women, IDUS account for 41 percent of such cases. Within this subgroup, gay/bisexual IDUS pose an especially high risk to themselves as well as their sexual partners as a result of risky behavior associated with intravenous drug use. Mexican-origin women who are in a relationship with an IDU are also at risk for HIV even if they themselves are not IDUS. In addition, those women who are IDUS are just as likely to engage in risky drug-related and sexual behavior as non-Hispanic white women, thus increasing their exposure to HIV/AIDS. Other adverse health effects associated with substance abuse among Mexican Americans include hepatitis B and C, cirrhosis of the liver, chronic liver disease, lung cancer, cardiovascular disease, and high mortality and injury rates due to motor vehicle accidents.

Prevention of drug use as a means of reducing the risk for HIV/AIDS in the overall Hispanic population should focus on increasing awareness of the risks involved in taking drugs and having unprotected sex. Preventive measures include disseminating information, particularly in programs aimed at Hispanic youth, providing social resistance skills training, and providing programs that are both culturally appropriate and culturally sensitive in their approaches to prevention strategies. Strategies may include providing information in Spanish, hiring **bilingual/bicultural** staff, aiming intervention at specific communities, recognizing cultural differences and values, and providing culturally sensitive health care environments. Although providing intervention programs to reduce substance abuse and associated health risks is a challenge, there are established models that can be used in constructing a program that provides culturally competent and culturally sensitive interventions.

■ Discussion Exercises

1. In what ways has HIV/AIDS affected the health status of the Mexican origin population? What types of prevention options have been presented in this chapter?

2. How does substance abuse among Mexican-origin persons differ from that of non-Hispanic whites, other Hispanic subpopulations, and African Americans?

3. What are the most common predictors of substance abuse among Mexican American adults and adolescents?

4. What types of drug-related behaviors pose the highest risks to the health status of the Mexican-origin community? How are Hispanic youth at risk?

5. Discuss the special health problems faced by Mexican-origin women.

6. How can cultural factors increase or decrease the risk for substance abuse? How can cultural concepts and beliefs be incorporated into substance abuse prevention and intervention programs?

■ Suggested Readings

Akins, C., and G. Beschner. *Ethnography: A Research Tool for Policy Makers in the Drug and Alcohol Fields.* Rockville, Md.: NIDA, 1980.

Botvin, G. J. "Drug Abuse Prevention in School Settings." Chap. 9 in *Drug Abuse Prevention with Multiethnic Youth,* eds. G. J. Botvin, S. Schinke, and M. A. Orlandi, pp. 169–92. Thousand Oaks, Calif.: Sage, 1995.

Bullington, B. M. *Heroin in the Barrio.* Lexington, Mass.: Lexington Press, 1977.

Felix-Ortiz, M., and M. D. Newcomb. "Cultural Identity and Drug Use among Latino and Latina Adolescents." Chap. 8 in *Drug Abuse Prevention with Multiethnic Youth,* eds. G. J. Botvin, S. Schinke, and M. A. Orlandi, pp. 147–68. Thousand Oaks, Calif.: Sage.

Glick, R., and J. Moore, eds. *Drug Use in Hispanic Communities.* New Brunswick, N.J.: Rutgers University Press, 1990.

Hanson, B. et al. *Life with Heroin: Voices from the Inner City.* Lexington, Mass.: Lexington Books, 1985.

Mondanaro, J. *Treating Chemically Dependent Women.* Lexington, Mass.: Lexington Books, 1988.

Moore, J. et al. *Homeboys: Gangs, Drugs and Prison in the Barrios of Los Angeles.* Philadelphia: Temple University Press, 1978.

Padilla, F. *The Gang as an American Enterprise.* Brunswick, N.J.: Rutgers University Press, 1992.

Robles, R. R. et al. "Effects of HIV Testing and Counseling on Reducing HIV Risk Behavior among Two Ethnic Groups." In *Multicultural AIDS Prevention Programs,* ed. R. Trotter. New York: Haworth Press, 1996.

Rogler, L. H. et al. "What Do Culturally Sensitive Mental Health Services Mean? The Case of Hispanics." *American Psychologist* 42 (1987), pp. 565–70.

Santisteban, D., and J. Szapocnik. *The Hispanic Substance Abuser: The Search for Prevention Strategies.* New York: Grune and Stratton, 1982.

Singer, M. et al. "AIDS and the IV Drug User: The Local Context in Prevention Efforts." In *Rethinking AIDS Prevention: Cultural Approaches,* eds. R. Bolton and M. Singer, pp. 147–68. New York: Gordon and Breach Science Publishers, 1992.

■ Notes

1. Many of the data in this section are for the Hispanic population because no data are available for the Mexican-origin subpopulation.

2. Centers for Disease Control and Prevention (CDC), *HIV/AIDS Surveillance Report* year-end edition, vol. 10, no. 2 (Washington, D.C.: U.S. Department of Health and Human Services, Public Health Service, December 1998).

3. *Youth Risk Behavior Survey* (Atlanta, Ga.: CDC, 1995).

4. L. D. Johnston, P. M. O'Malley, and J. G. Bachman, *The Monitoring the Future Study, 1975–1998,* vol. 1 (Washington, D.C.: National Institute on Drug Abuse, U.S. Department of Health and Human Services, National Institutes of Health, 1999).

5. National Institute on Drug Abuse (NIDA), *National Household Survey on Drug Abuse: Population Estimates 1991,* DHHS Pub. No. (ADM) 92-1887 (Washington, D.C.: U.S. Department of Health and Human Services, 1991).

6. NIDA, *Use of Selected Drugs among Hispanics: Mexican-Americans, Puerto Ricans, and Cuban-Americans. Findings from the Hispanic Health and Nutrition Examination Survey* (Washington, D.C.: U.S. Department of Health and Human Services, Public Health Service, 1987).

7. *Youth Risk Behavior Survey.*

8. NIDA, *National Household Survey on Drug Abuse.*

9. NIDA, *Use of Selected Drugs among Hispanics.*

10. H. M. Ginzburg, "Intravenous Drug Users and the Acquired Immune Deficiency Syndrome," *Public Health Reports* 99 (1984), pp. 206–12.

11. NIDA, *National Household Survey on Drug Abuse.*

12. Ibid.

13. Impact Consultants, *School-Based Survey Report for 6th and 10th graders in Yuma County, Arizona, 1995* (Tucson, Ariz.: Impact Consultants, 1995).

14. Johnston, O'Malley, and Bachman, *The Monitoring the Future Study.*

15. Impact Consultants, *School Based Survey Report.*

16. NIDA, *National Household Survey on Drug Abuse.*

17. *Youth Risk Behavior Survey.*

18. M. Felix-Ortiz and M. D. Newcomb, "Cultural Identity and Drug Use among Latino and Latina Adolescents," chap. 8 in *Drug Abuse Prevention with Multiethnic Youth,* eds. G. J. Botvin, S. Schinke, and M. A. Orlandi, pp. 147–68 (Thousand Oaks, Calif.: Sage, 1995).

19. Ibid., p. 150.

20. E. L. Chávez, R. Edwards, and E. R. Oetting, "Mexican American and White American Dropouts' Drug Use, Health Status, and Involvement in Violence," *Public Health Reports* 104, no. 6 (1986), pp. 594–604.

21. CDC, *HIV/AIDS Surveillance Report.*

22. COSSMHO (National Coalition of Hispanic Health and Human Service Organizations), *HIV/AIDS—The Impact on Hispanics in Selected States* (Washington, D.C.: COSSMHO, 1991).

23. A. L. Estrada, "Drug Use and HIV Risks among African American, Mexican American, and Puerto Rican Drug Injectors," *Journal of Psychoactive Drugs* 30, no. 3 (1998), pp. 247–53; see also I. D. Montoya, A. L. Estrada, A. Jones, and R. R. Robles, "An Analysis of Differential Factors Affecting Risk Behaviors among Out-of-Treatment Drug Users in Four Cities," *Drugs and Society* 9 (1996), pp. 155–71; and R. R. Robles, T. D. Matos, H. M. Colon, et al., "Effects of HIV Testing and Counseling on Reducing HIV Risk Behavior among Two Ethnic Groups," in *Multicultural AIDS Prevention Programs,* ed. R. Trotter (New York: Haworth Press, 1996).

24. A. L. Estrada, et al., "HIV Risk Behaviors among Mexican-Origin and Anglo Female Intravenous Drug Users," *Border Health* 7, no. 1 (1991), pp. 1–4.

25. Estrada, "Drug Use and HIV Risks."

26. R. E. Booth et al., "HIV Risk-Related Sex Behaviors among Injection Drug Users, Crack Smokers, and Injection Drug Users Who Smoke Crack," *American Journal of Public Health* 83, no. 8 (1993), pp. 1144–48; see also J. B. Cohen, et al., "Women and IV Drugs: Parental and Heterosexual Transmission of Human Immunodeficiency Virus, *Journal of Drug Issues* 19, no. 1 (1989), pp. 39–56; A. L. Estrada, "Behavioral Epidemiology of HIV Risks among Injection Drug Users: Comparative Assessment." Paper presented to the HIV-AIDS Health Services Research and Delivery Conference, Agency for Health Care Policy and Research (AHCPR) Miami, Fla., December 1991.

27. A. L. Estrada, J. R. Erickson, S. J. Stevens, and P. J. Glider, "AIDS Risk Behaviors

among Straight and Gay IVDUs: A Comparative Analysis." Paper presented at the Second Annual National AIDS Demonstration and Research (NADR) Conference, Bethesda, Md., November 1990.

28. D. A. Dawson and A. M. Hardy, "AIDS Knowledge and Attitudes among Hispanic Americans: Provisional Data from the 1988 National Health Interview Survey," NCHS Advance Data 166 (1990), pp. 1–22; see also R. J. DiClemente, C. B. Boyer, and E. S. Morales, "Minorities and AIDS: Knowledge, Attitudes, and Misconceptions among Black and Hispanic Adolescents," American Journal of Public Health 78, no. 1 (1988), pp. 55–57; R. Hingson et al., "Survey of AIDS Knowledge and Behavior Changes among Massachusetts Adults," Preventive Medicine 18 (1989), pp. 806–16.

29. J. A. Flora and C. E. Thoresen, "Reducing the Risk of AIDS in Adolescents," American Psychologist 43, no. 11 (1988), pp. 965–70.

30. S. M. Kegeles et al., "Sexually Active Adolescents and Condoms: Changes over One Year in Knowledge, Attitudes, and Use," American Journal of Public Health 78 (1988), pp. 460–61.

31. S. M. Davis and M. B. Harris, "Sexual Knowledge, Sexual Interests, and Sources of Sexual Information of Rural and Urban Adolescents from Three Cultures," Adolescence 17, no. 66 (1982), pp. 471–92.

32. D. S. Moore and P. I. Erickson, "Age, Gender, and Ethnic Differences in Sexual and Contraceptive Knowledge, Attitudes, and Behaviors," Family and Community Health 8 (1985), pp. 38–51.

33. D. C. Des Jarlais et al., "Heterosexual Partners: A Large Risk Group for AIDS" [letter], Lance 2, no. 8415 (1984), pp. 1346–47.

34. J. Mondanaro, Treating Chemically Dependent Women (Lexington, Mass.: Lexington Books, 1988).

35. G. Weissman et al., "Drug Use and Sexual Behaviors among Sex Partners of Injecting-Drug Users, United States, 1988–1990," Mortality and Morbidity Weekly Report 40, no. 49 (1991), pp. 855–60.

36. S. J. Stevens, J. R. Erickson, and A. L. Estrada, "Characteristics of Female Sexual Partners of Injection Drug Users in Southern Arizona: Implications for Effective HIV Risk Reduction Interventions," Drugs and Society 7, no. 3/4 (1993), pp. 129–42.

37. Substance Abuse and Mental Health Services Administration (SAMHSA), Data from the Drug Abuse Warning Network (DAWN), 1994 data file (Rockville, Md.: SAMHSA, 1994).

38. Felix-Ortiz and Newcomb, "Cultural Identity and Drug Use among Latino and Latina Adolescents."

39. G. J. Botvin, "Drug Abuse Prevention in School Settings," chap. 9 in Drug Abuse Prevention with Multiethnic Youth, eds. G. J. Botvin, S. Schinke, and M. A. Orlandi, pp. 169–92 (Thousand Oaks, Calif.: Sage, 1995).

40. Ibid.

4

"Treated like second-class citizens"

HEALTH CARE ACCESS

There was no medical insurance in my family . . . Grandma would pay. At that time we had doctors that did home visits. As a matter of fact, I remember having an asthma attack and the doctor coming to visit me. (María L., 44)

I initially told [the doctor] that I was on AHCCCS[1] because of the circumstance, not by choice, that I was a professional and that I was used to having my own medical insurance, because somehow I felt that I would be treated differently [than a non-AHCCCS patient] . . . and I feel that I was right . . . the impression I had about AHCCCS patients . . . is that they are [treated like] second-class citizens. (Carmen G., 49)

Like many **Mexican Americans**, both María and Carmen experienced the dilemma of not having health insurance or the security of private health insurance coverage. As a child growing up in San Diego, California, María and her family did not have health insurance, and therefore had to rely on her grandmother to pay for the family's health care. Carmen's case illustrates the problem of losing health insurance due to unforeseen circumstances. She was forced to give up her job, resulting in the loss of her private health coverage, and move from Colorado back to Arizona to care for her ailing mother. These two women clearly illustrate the dilemmas of **financial access** to health care; that is, having either private or public health insurance to pay for medical services. This problem is widespread and often linked to employment factors such as **occupational location** (including economic sector and business size), part-time versus full-time status, and salary. Therefore, the issue of medical coverage for this group is often defined by the lack of financial access. Before examining the specific coverage problems faced by the Mexican-origin population, we must define **health care access.**

■ What Is Health Care Access?

The issue of health care access is significant to the **health status** of all Mexican Americans. Aspects that specifically affect this population include financial access to care, geographic access to care, access to timely care, having a regular source of care, access to culturally and linguistically appropriate care, and access to specialized types of health care. In many respects, we can divide access issues for the Mexican-origin population into two broad categories: (1) financial access to care and (2) access to culturally and linguistically competent health care professionals that serve predominately Mexican-origin communities. The latter point also encompasses the issues of location of delivery and timely and appropriate care. As we will see later in this chapter, access to a regular source of care for minority populations is linked to the availability of minority health professionals in local areas.

Health care access is important because it influences health status and quality of life. According to Williams and Torrens, "Poor access may be reflected in delayed care seeking, absence of preventive care, and low patient satisfaction."[2] These problems are illustrated by Carmen's loss of private health insurance, which affected not only her health but also the quality of health care she received:

> Prior to the last six months I did have medical insurance available to me because, of course, I was working. I would definitely say that since January of this year, not having had medical insurance until May definitely affected my health because my body became weaker and weaker. . . . It's such a shame because medicine is supposed to be all about healing and helping and it's turned into such a money monopoly. (Carmen G., 49)

Unfortunately, Carmen's sentiments and experiences are all too familiar to Mexican Americans. For this population, lack of health care coverage and access is a barrier preventing many from obtaining a regular source of care that provides routine checkups and timely treatment of illnesses and diseases. Another concern is the shortage of health care professionals knowledgeable in managing treatment for **Hispanics**. As we will discover later in this chapter, the shortage of Hispanic, particularly Mexican American, health care professionals limits access to care for this group. The cost of care also increases as Mexican-origin persons who are denied access to regular care must seek treatment in hospital emergency rooms when an illness has become unmanageable or life-threatening. These costs are paid by the state in the case of public health insurance and by the individual in the case of private insurance or no insurance.[3] This problem is often exacerbated because of the use of alternative forms of treatment either prior to or in place of consulting a physician. For example, in the border region, Mexican-origin persons may receive health care in neighboring Mexican states, which lowers their out-of-pocket expenses or enables them to self-medicate by using pharmaceuticals that do not require a prescription.

■ Who Are the Uninsured?

In the United States, more than 43 million Americans are without any form of health insurance; slightly more than 10 million of these uninsured are children under eighteen years of age.[4] Although more **non-Hispanic** than Hispanic whites are uninsured, the Hispanic population has a disproportionate percentage of uninsured: Hispanics comprise roughly 11 percent of the entire U.S. population under age sixty-five, yet they make up 20 percent of the uninsured population. In contrast, non-Hispanic whites represent 75 percent of the U.S. population under age sixty-five but make up only 62 percent of Americans with no health insurance.[5] Another way to examine the same data is by examining the percentage of uninsured within each ethnic and racial group. Within the three major ethnic and racial categories, Hispanics are disproportionately uninsured: One-third of all Hispanics do not have any form of health insurance, compared to one-fifth of all African Americans and one-seventh of all non-Hispanic whites.

Financial Access to Care: A Crisis for Mexican-Origin Patients

> I was sick one time for five years because I had blood coming out of my mouth. For a lot of years I didn't know why it was coming out. I used to have a health plan maybe ten years ago. . . . I had a sore throat for two years, and it wasn't until I went to a county facility that the doctor explained to me that I had acid reflux. (Danny F., 36)

The issue of financial access to adequate health insurance is the major focus of discussion within the domain of health care coverage for many

Hispanics, particularly the Mexican-origin population. Inability to pay is the most significant barrier to a regular source of health care for this group. Because uninsured individuals must pay for the cost of care out-of-pocket, they underutilize preventive services and delay treatment for both chronic and life-threatening conditions. Danny's case shows the impact of lack of financial access to health care over a long period of time. The problem he was diagnosed with, acid reflux, is an easily treatable gastrointestinal problem. Early diagnosis and treatment would have improved his quality of life and prevented his costly use of **patchwork providers** (those that treat the underinsured or uninsured), a method commonly used by the uninsured and underinsured in California to treat various medical conditions. While Danny's experience is not unique, it illustrates the problems resulting from a health care financing and delivery system that is based on the employment status of the individual.

Private Health Insurance: An Employer-Based Model

As the cost of health care, particularly for care resulting from catastrophic illnesses, exceeds the price that most Americans are able to pay, health insurance becomes vital in ensuring quality of life and continuity of health care services. Without private or public health insurance, individuals may be denied treatment or services except in medical emergencies, which can result in long-term damage to their health.

Most Americans obtain access to health insurance through the workplace. Employers, particularly large firms and the public sector (including government), typically provide health insurance to an individual and his or her family members as part of a comprehensive benefit package. This type of coverage is known as a **voluntary system of health insurance**. An individual employee either shares the **health insurance premium** with the employer or is provided with coverage at no cost. This coverage usually extends to the employee's family for a relatively small increase in cost, which is usually paid through regular premiums. In general, access to private health insurance is linked to the type, site, and duration of employment. These factors significantly influence the profile of uninsured Americans. For example, companies that provide full-coverage health insurance tend to be large private and public employers. The private sector includes corporations and businesses; the public sector includes school districts, universities, and governmental (or quasi-governmental) entities. Employers that do not typically provide health insurance to their employees include small businesses in competitive markets such as landscaping; self-employed professionals such as lawyers, accountants, independent contractors, and consultants; and those who employ persons such as domestic workers or child-care providers. This type of employment frequently limits access to private insurance, as small employers often cannot afford to pay the health insurance premium to cover the cost of an employee's health insurance.

The Public Sector: Limited Access to
Public-Sector Health Insurance

> The hours I work do not qualify me for part-time status to get part-time benefits, so therefore I didn't qualify to receive health insurance. . . . In February of this year, I twisted my knee and I was barely able to walk on it, but was hesitant to have anybody look at it because of the cost of not having any insurance. . . . Had I gone to the hospital and had X-rays taken and everything else, then I would have this thousand-dollar, if not more, medical bill that I could not pay for. So that's why not having health insurance has prevented me from seeking medical attention. (Marissia Q., 22)

The welfare reform act recently passed by Congress has brought significant changes in publicly subsidized services for the poor and **medically indigent**. Yet, even before these changes, the Mexican-origin population in the United States did not use public health insurance programs as much as other racial and ethnic groups did. This may be due in part to the fact that a significant percentage of the Mexican-origin population is composed of recent **immigrants**, whose status affects their eligibility for federally subsidized health care. Another factor limiting the health care access of recent immigrants is their unfamiliarity with the availability of these programs. Moreover, in many of the states where the majority of the Mexican-origin population resides, there are stringent income eligibility requirements in addition to county or state requirements that limit access to these public programs. Thus, factors such as low income, citizenship status, regional differences in eligibility requirements for publicly subsidized programs, and limited outreach to eligible individuals within this ethnic group combine to produce low enrollment rates for Mexican-origin persons in public programs that provide financial coverage for health care services.

The impact of immigrant status on the use of publicly subsidized health insurance is illustrated in table 4.1. Mexican immigrants' use of Medicaid

Table 4.1 Medicaid Coverage by Population Group, 1999 (Ages 1–64)

	NONCITIZENS (%)	NATURALIZED CITIZENS (%)	NATIVE-BORN (%)
Black	10	7	23
Mexican	9	9	20
Other Hispanic	9	7	22
Asian/Pacific Islander	8	5	13
White	8	3	6

Source: U.S. Bureau of the Census, Current Population Survey, March 1999 Sample W. (Washington, D.C.: Government Printing Office, 1999).

during 1999 follows a pattern similar to that of other groups of immigrants. However, the percentages of noncitizen and naturalized Mexican immigrants receiving Medicaid is less than half the percentage of Mexican Americans. Thus, based on these data, immigration status plays an important role in the use of Medicaid within the Mexican-origin population.

Medicaid, Medicare, and SSI: A Brief Overview

Three major federal health care programs target people who are medically at-risk, disabled, or elderly. These are Medicaid, **Supplemental Security Income** (ssi), and **Medicare**. ssi is "a nationwide federal assistance program administered by the Social Security Administration (ssa) that guarantees a minimum level of income for needy aged, blind, or disabled individuals."[6]

Given the youthful character and relatively large family size of Mexican Americans, Medicaid eligibility criteria are of great interest in the examination of the group's overall health care access. According to the Health Care Financing Administration: "Medicaid is a jointly funded, federal-state health insurance program for certain low-income and needy people. It covers approximately 36 million individuals including children; the aged, blind, and/or disabled; and people who are eligible to receive federally assisted income maintenance payments."[7] The groups covered under Medicaid include pregnant women, children, the elderly, and the disabled.

Although this working definition applies to the general application of this program, each state has discretion in determining eligibility. However, there are requirements that states must meet in order to obtain eligible Medicaid funds from the federal government. For example "states are required to provide Medicaid coverage for most individuals who receive

Table 4.2 Medicaid Eligibility Requirements for Pregnant Women in Southwestern States, 1999

STATE	INCOME REQUIREMENT	ADDITIONAL REQUIREMENTS
Arizona (AHCCCS/SOBRA)	140% of FPL[1] or less	Social Security Number, U.S. citizen or qualified alien
California (Medi-Cal)	200% of FPL or less	Must be state resident; for undocumented immigrants/refugees: 133% or less of AFDC[2] payment level
Colorado (BCKC adult)	133% of FPL or less	Income can exceed AFDC need standards
New Mexico	185% of FPL or less	U.S. citizen or qualified alien, coverage ends two months after delivery; family planning services are available for twenty-four months after delivery
Texas	185% or less of FPL	Those with incomes below 133% of maximum TANF grant are eligible as "medically needy," coverage ends two months after delivery

1. The Federal Poverty Line (FPL) is the guideline for determining poverty status in the United States. The yearly income limit for a family of four to be in poverty is $16,700 in the forty-eight states and the District of Columbia.
2. AFDC is Aid for Families with Dependent Children, which is another federally subsidized program for the poor.

Sources: Arizona Health Care Cost Containment System web site: http://170.68.21.47/Content/ Resources/AnnRpt97/appendix/apndxB.htm; Medi-Cal: personal communication from C. Page, 7/12/99; Colorado Department of Health Care Policy and Financing web site:www.chcpf.state.co.us/refmat/99RefMan-3.html#EES-6; New Mexico Human Services Department: personal communication from L. Martínez, 11/5/99; Texas Department of Human Services web site: www.dhs.state.tx.us/programs/TexasWorks/pregnant.html; Department of Health and Human Services web site: http://aspe.os.dhhs.gov/poverty/99poverty.htm.

federally assisted income maintenance payments, as well as Supplemental Security Income (SSI) for related groups not receiving cash payments." This would include, for example, individuals that receive SSI and "infants born to Medicaid-eligible pregnant women."[8]

States have some discretion in determining the level of coverage based on their willingness to subsidize the health insurance program targeted to the poor and medically indigent. This has resulted in regional differences that may partially explain why the Mexican-origin population has differential access to publicly subsidized health insurance. Table 4.2 lists the Medicaid eligibility requirements for pregnant women in the five southwestern states. It is a good example of the diversity of state requirements for a targeted group within the Medicaid population.

For example, pregnant women in Arizona and Colorado must be poorer than women in California and New Mexico in order to qualify for Medicaid coverage. In addition, the importance of proving legal status varies by state, thus affecting access for the undocumented immigrant population. The more generous eligibility requirements and coverage in states such as California should provide greater financial access to Hispanics. However, even with more generous coverage based on a higher poverty threshold, the citizenship status of Mexican immigrants influences the accessibility of publicly subsidized health insurance for the poor members of this **subpopulation**. In California, beginning with the passage of the 1994 voter initiative **Proposition 187**, which attempted to limit access to publicly subsidized health care services for undocumented immigrants, the state has been engaged in a debate over which health care services, if any, should be provided to undocumented immigrants. There has been increased interest in curbing the access of recent immigrants to social services, including publicly subsidized health care programs such as Medicaid. With the advent of welfare reform at the federal level, there have also been serious attempts in Congress to restrict the eligibility of *legal* immigrants for entitlement programs such as Medicaid. The rising costs of these programs, as well as the goal of decreasing the welfare rolls as mandated under welfare reform, provide an impetus for considering the removal of legal immigrants from the eligibility pool. Thus, even in states with relatively generous eligibility requirements, the relation of citizenship status to health care access has become a serious issue given popular sentiment to deny most state benefits to nonlegal, and even legal, residents.

Medicare is a federal public health insurance program that was created primarily for the elderly. It covers people who are sixty-five years of age or older, individuals with permanent kidney failure, and certain people with disabilities. Unlike Medicaid, there is no income or eligibility means test for this program. Entitlement is based on employee payment into the Medicare trust. To qualify for Medicare, either the individual or his/her spouse must work for a minimum of ten years in a Medicare-covered job and be a permanent resident or citizen.[9] In some respects, Medicare may be viewed as a universal insurance program for America's senior citizens. There are two parts to the Medicare program. Medicare Part A, which covers most of the U.S. population ages sixty-five and older, is known as hospital insurance and provides the following benefits: ninety days of **inpatient care**, sixty reserve inpatient days for individuals who exhaust their ninety days, one hundred days of care in a skilled nursing facility after leaving the hospital, and **home health agency** visits. Part B of the Medicare program is a supplemental health insurance program paid for through monthly premiums. It covers physician services, **outpatient health services**, and home health care for those not covered by Part A.[10]

 ## Risk Factors That Influence the Health Insurance Coverage of the Mexican-Origin Population

Much of the Mexican-origin population falls within the category of the **working poor**. This means that their incomes do not meet the **federal poverty levels** required for publicly subsidized health insurance but they are employed in low-wage employment sectors that do not provide health insurance. Compounding this problem, the Mexican-origin population sixty-five years of age and older has a very low rate of private health insurance coverage provided through previous employment, leaving them entirely dependent on Medicare.

Occupational Location

Occupational location refers to the type of job and economic sector in which a person is employed. At the low end of the spectrum are low-status, low-wage jobs such as those in the agricultural and service sectors, while at the high end are corporate executives, doctors, lawyers, and other white-collar jobs. Compared to blacks, white non-Hispanics, Asians, and other Hispanics, the Mexican-origin population under age sixty-five had the lowest rate of private insurance obtained through employment (see table 4.3). Given the low occupational status of a large percentage of the Mexican-origin population of the United States, particularly in the Southwest, it is not surprising that private health insurance coverage is relatively low.

Despite having low rates of private health insurance coverage, many Mexican-origin workers are unable to obtain publicly subsidized health insurance because they do not qualify based on their income levels. A recent study by the Center on Budget and Policy Priorities demonstrates why the

Table 4.3 Percentage of Population under Age Sixty-Five Having Private Insurance Coverage Obtained through the Workplace, 1994–1996

RACE/ETHNICITY	1994	1995	1996
White, non-Hispanic	70.4	72.1	71.5
Black, non-Hispanic	49.2	50.9	52.2
Asian/Pacific Islander	57.4	59.8	59.3
All Hispanic	44.5	44.0	43.8
Mexican	43.7	41.9	40.9

Source: National Center for Health Statistics, *Health, United States, 1998,* table 133 (Hyattsville, Md.: U.S. Department of Health and Human Services, 1998).

working poor do not have health insurance. A simple example should help illuminate this problem. Texas, for instance, requires a very low income level in order to qualify for publicly supported health insurance such as Medicaid. In Texas, if a three-person household (e.g., mother, father, one child) earns more than $336.00 per month, their income would be considered too high to qualify for publicly subsidized medical insurance. This means that a family member or members could work no more than a total of sixteen hours a week at $5.25 per hour (the minimum wage) to qualify for Medicaid coverage. Working couples with children face a dilemma in that they are often worse off in terms of eligibility for publicly subsidized health insurance than single head-of-household families with children. Although children in these working poor families may be covered under publicly funded health insurance programs, the parents may have limited or no access to publicly supported health insurance programs.[11]

Eligibility Issues for Seniors

As illustrated in table 4.4, the Mexican-origin population sixty-five years of age and older has a very low rate of private health insurance coverage provided through previous employment programs, compared to white and black non-Hispanics. The significance of this situation is that, unlike the 40 percent of non-Hispanic whites who have private health insurance to complement or replace their Medicare coverage, most of the senior Mexican-origin population must rely on Medicare to cover the bulk of their health care costs. This is also a manifestation of their occupational location during their prime working years in low-wage and low-benefit sectors of the economy. This group of seniors generally has no coverage for prescription

Table 4.4 Percentage of Population Age Sixty-Five and Older Having Private Insurance Coverage Obtained through the Workplace, 1994–1996

RACE/ETHNICITY	1994	1995	1996
White, non-Hispanic	43.8	42.9	40.8
Black, non-Hispanic	26.8	26.1	30.7
Asian/Pacific Islander	27.3	27.2	13.1
All Hispanic	22.1	20.1	19.4
Mexican	23.1	17.4	18.7

Source: National Center for Health Statistics, *Health, United States, 1998,* table 134 (Hyattsville, Md.: U.S. Department of Health and Human Services, 1998).

drugs and other medical expenses not covered under Medicare. Lack of supplemental insurance places an enormous financial burden on these low-income seniors, who have fixed incomes from Social Security or private pension plans. Because of the substantial out-of-pocket expenses, many do not follow through with regular treatment or medications for common chronic conditions such as diabetes, high blood pressure, or heart disease.

Mexican-Origin Women: A Group at Risk

[The lack of access] is reflected in very low levels of utilization of screening technologies among women (e.g. **Pap smear**, mammography, etc.). . . . An understanding of the **epidemiology** and biology of many disease processes (e.g., cervical cancer and HPV disease) in high-risk populations would greatly advance our understanding of these illnesses. (Francisco G., M.D., 35)

A significant number of Mexican-origin women either are not able to work full time because of family obligations or are employed in low-wage sectors. As a result they do not have access to health insurance. This is illustrated in table 4.5, which shows the percentage who have private health insurance or Medicaid.

With the exception of those in their thirties, more than one-third of Mexican-origin women do not have any source of payment for their health care. These data become even more alarming when we review women who are no longer in their childbearing years but are not old enough to qualify for Medicare. Many chronic health conditions, such as diabetes and cardiovascular disease, manifest themselves after age forty, but women in this age bracket who lack health insurance cannot receive timely screening

Table 4.5 Percentage of Mexican-Origin Women Having Health Insurance Coverage or Medicaid Card (n = 2,142)

AGE DECADE (years)	PERCENTAGE
20–29	62.8
30–39	70.6
40–49	63.1
50–64	58.3

Source: A. R. de la Torre, R. Friis, H. R. Hunter, and L. García, "The Health Insurance Status of U.S. Latino Women: A Profile from the 1982–84 Hispanic HANES," American Journal of Public Health 86, no. 4 (1996), p. 534.

and monitoring of these diseases to minimize their adverse health effects. Moreover, older uninsured women are at greater risk of remaining undiagnosed and untreated for life-threatening diseases such as breast and cervical cancer that have few early symptoms. Thus, the poor health status of these women can be directly linked to their lack of financial access to health insurance.[12]

Occupational location is a key factor in the lack of health insurance for Mexican-origin women, in that many of these women are located in low-wage job sectors. There are also other factors that influence their lack of coverage, however. Marital status, poverty, education, and levels of **acculturation** correlate with health insurance status. For example, a married woman is more likely to have health insurance through her husband's employment. If she speaks Spanish and identifies herself as a Mexican rather than a Mexican American or **Chicana**, she is less likely to have health insurance. Finally, both her educational level and whether she is above or below the federal poverty level will greatly influence whether she has financial access to health care through the voluntary health insurance market. In addition, culturally defined gender roles in the household may limit Mexican-origin women's employment prospects, as do life cycle decisions such as pregnancy and child rearing. These decisions can interrupt employment and affect the choice of whether to work. The ability of recently immigrated women to adapt to the institutional environment and bureaucratic health care system of the United States also places real constraints on access to public and private health insurance. Thus, for Mexican-origin women, the issue of health care access goes beyond a simple model linked to employment to encompass broader social issues that are defined by their

Table 4.6 Undocumented Latino/a Immigrants by Country of Origin and Population Size

COUNTRY OF ORIGIN	U.S. POPULATION SIZE
Mexico	2,700,000
El Salvador	335,000
Guatemala	165,000
Honduras	90,000
Nicaragua	70,000
Colombia	65,000
Ecuador	55,000
Dominican Republic	50,000
Peru	30,000

Source: Immigration and Naturalization Service, "Illegal Alien Resident Population," available from Immigration and Naturalization Service web site: www.ins.usdoj.gov/graphics/as/statistics/illegalalien/index.htm.

immigrant status, marital status, and other factors.[13] Recognition of these gender differences is an important step in targeting health coverage strategies for uninsured and underinsured Mexican-origin women.

Undocumented Mexican-Origin Immigrants

A small yet important group within the immigrant population is composed of undocumented immigrants of Mexican origin. Currently, there are an estimated five million undocumented immigrants in the United States. Of this number almost three quarters are of **Latino/a** origin. Most are concentrated in specific regions of the country, primarily in the Northeast, the Southeast, and the Southwest. In the Southwest, the state with the highest number of undocumented immigrants is California, where 40 percent of all U.S. undocumented immigrants reside.

Mexico is the country of origin of more than half of all undocumented immigrants. While the term "Latino/Latina" is used to describe undocumented immigrants in some reports, approximately 80 percent of all Latino/a undocumented immigrants are of Mexican origin. Therefore, the use of the Latino/a ethnic designation may not be very useful when describing undocumented immigrants. We recommend population-specific terms that are based on country of origin. The fact that Mexicans are overwhelmingly represented within the Latino/a undocumented immigrant group can be seen in table 4.6.

The largest portion of the undocumented population is located in the

Table 4.7 Undocumented Immigrant Population in the Southwest

STATE OF RESIDENCE	POPULATION
California	2,000,000
Texas	700,000
Arizona	115,000
Colorado	45,000
New Mexico	37,000

Source: Immigration and Naturalization Service, "Illegal Alien Resident Population," available from Immigration and Naturalization Service web site: www.ins.usdoj.gov/graphics/as/statistics/illegalalien/index.htm.

Southwest; a state-by-state breakdown is provided in table 4.7. One can easily understand how the proximity of Mexico, as well as the large Mexican-origin population in these states, serves as a magnet for undocumented immigration. However location and ethnic concentration are insufficient to explain the overrepresentation of undocumented immigrants in the Southwest. A primary reason why undocumented workers from Mexico are lured to the Southwest is the large demand for low-wage labor in service-sector industries and agriculture. This "pull" to the United States is further exacerbated by the "push" from Mexico's less-developed economy, where the average daily wage is significantly lower than that paid in the United States. For example, the Mexican minimum wage in U.S. dollars is $3.40 per day compared to the U.S. minimum wage, which is $5.25 per hour, or $42.00 per day before taxes.[14]

The fact that many undocumented workers are employed in low-wage sectors of the U.S. economy has direct implications for their access to adequate health care and health insurance. Most are employed in sectors that offer no health insurance to employees, thus they have no access to health care except for emergency services. Moreover, because they have immigrated without documentation, most avoid seeking health care except in emergencies for fear of detection and deportation by the Immigration and Naturalization Service (INS), often referred to as *La Migra*. This situation is illustrated in table 4.8, which shows the percentage and insurance status of undocumented Mexican-origin immigrants in Fresno and Los Angeles counties, California, which have large Mexican-origin populations.[15]

According to a study by the Project HOPE Center for Health Affairs, this low rate of coverage presents problems such as lower use of private physi-

Table 4.8 Health Insurance Status of Undocumented Mexican-Origin Immigrants in Los Angeles and Fresno Counties (under Sixty-Five Years of Age)

COUNTY	UNINSURED (%)	PUBLIC INSURANCE (%)	PRIVATE INSURANCE (%)
Los Angeles	84	12	4
Fresno	68	27	5

Source: Immigration and Naturalization Service, "Illegal Alien Resident Population," available from Immigration and Naturalization Service web site: www.ins.usdoj.gov/graphics/as/statistics/illegalalien/index.htm.

cian services compared to legal immigrants, and greater reliance on local clinics and health centers for primary care needs. In addition, the second most likely site of care for undocumented immigrants is in the emergency room, which is a costly alternative for treatment. This study also suggests that because of the high poverty rates of undocumented immigrants, they may have lower expectations for care and be unable to pay for services, which may explain their underutilization of health care services. Finally, undocumented immigrants are not eligible for income support programs such as Aid to Families with Dependent Children (AFDC), Medicaid, and Food Stamp programs, so they have few alternatives within the U.S. social service system. Unlike other large Latino/a subpopulations, such as Puerto Rican and Cuban Americans, the issue of legal status is an important health care policy issue in the case of Mexican-origin immigrants. This differential treatment is due to the proximity of Mexico to the United States, the historical exploitation of cheap Mexican labor in the Southwest and elsewhere, and the regional concentration of undocumented Mexican immigrants in states such as California. Even though the number of undocumented immigrants is relatively small compared to legal Mexican immigrants and Mexican Americans, the continued presence of undocumented Mexican-origin persons, and the political backlash of the white electorate, require special consideration in addressing access issues for this group.

The Role of Minority Health Care Professionals in Access to Care

The health of minority populations will continue to lag behind as long as we continue to be underrepresented in the health professions. Mexican American communities have a dearth of providers. This proves to be a deterrent to access for many potential health care consumers. . . . The perspective of the Hispanic physician and scientist, at the bedside and at the lab bench, is crucial for the well-being of the entire community. (Francisco G., M.D., 35)

The pool of minority health care professionals (such as physicians, nurses, dentists, and physical therapists) is another significant issue affecting health care access. The shortage of Hispanic health care professionals limits access to health care for the Mexican American population because minority health professionals overwhelmingly serve in their respective communities. Most of these communities are poor and are underserved because of a low ratio of health professionals to this population. According to a Council on Graduate Medical Education report entitled "Minorities in Medicine" (May 1998), Hispanic health care professionals are important because they bridge the gap between the culture of the minority group and that of health care service providers. The report concluded that:

1. Minority physicians practice in medically underserved areas at almost twice the rate of non-minority physicians.
2. Minority patients were four times more likely than majority white patients to receive their health care services from nonwhite physicians than from white physicians.
3. Compared to the service areas for non-Hispanic physicians, there are twice as many Hispanic residents in the areas where Hispanic physicians practice.
4. Hispanic physicians provide health care to three times as many Hispanic patients as do non-Hispanic physicians.[16]

Thus, Hispanic physicians, like other minority physicians, provide greater access to care. Not only do they locate their practices where there are more Hispanic residents, but they actually serve more Hispanic patients relative to their non-Hispanic physician counterparts.

Given the documented evidence of the important role of minority physicians, the **American Association of Medical Colleges** (AAMC) in 1991 launched a major program known as "Project 3000 by 2000." Its goal was to increase the percentage of minority matriculation in **allopathic** medical schools to 19 percent of total **matriculants**. This percentage reflects the proportion of minorities in the total U.S. population in the year 2000. The

Table 4.9 National Medical School Applicant Pool, 1997: Selected Groups

APPLICANTS	APPLIED	ACCEPTED	ENROLLED	PERCENTAGE DROP IN APPLICANTS
White	26,295	10,899	10,504	8.7
African American	3,133	1,200	1,153	9.2
Mexican American	796	405	400	13.8

Source: Association of American Medical Colleges, *Facts: Applicants, Matriculants, and Graduates, 1991–1997,* U.S. 1997/1998 ed. (Washington, D.C.: Association of American Medical Colleges, 1998).

number of minority medical students needed in these medical schools to reach parity within the U.S. population by 2000 was 3,000.[17] Unfortunately, the AAMC's goal was not met, primarily because of a strong anti-affirmative-action movement that swept the United States during the 1990s. For example, in California, **Proposition 209** ended affirmative action in all public institutions, particularly the University of California system. The **Hopwood decision** in Texas also targeted affirmative action programs in higher education, lowering the number of minority applicants to medical and other health professional schools.

In the case of Mexican American physicians, the minority underrepresentation resulting from attacks on affirmative action programs becomes immediately apparent early on in the **educational pipeline**. Few medical school applicants are of Mexican descent and even fewer are accepted into medical schools. Although other minority groups face the same situation, it is disproportionately severe for Mexican-origin applicants given the small number of applicants to begin with (see table 4.9.)[18]

The percentage of Mexican-origin women in medical schools is also small. Unlike the case of African American women, who represent 61 percent of the total African American matriculants in medical school, Mexican-origin women follow a similar pattern as white non-Hispanic women with respect to representation. As illustrated in table 4.10, there is a clear need to increase the number of both Mexican American men and women in the medical profession. The table also illustrates the crisis in meeting the goal of "Project 3000 by 2000." By 1998, there were only 1,811 African American and Mexican American first-year students in U.S. medical schools, far below the stated goal of 3,000. Even with the support of the AAMC, the most powerful voice of U.S. medical colleges, meeting the needs

Table 4.10 First-Year Medical Students, 1997–1998: Selected Racial/Ethnic Groups

RACE/ETHNICITY	MEN	WOMEN	TOTAL
African American	525 (39%)	822 (61%)	1,347
Mexican American	262 (56%)	202 (44%)	464
White non-Hispanic and Foreign Students	6,549 (59%)	4,585 (41%)	11,134
Total (all groups)[1]	**9,519 (57%)**	**7,325 (43%)**	**16,844**

1. The total for all groups includes the total number of other Hispanic and non-Hispanic minority groups that are not listed in this table.

Source: Barzansky, B., H. S. Jonas, and S. I. Etzel, "Education Programs in U.S. Medical Schools, 1997–1998," *Journal of the American Medical Association* 280 (1998), pp. 803–8.

of minority communities has not been possible through the educational pipeline.

An important model in tackling the problem of underrepresentation via the educational pipeline is the federal program known as the Hispanic Centers of Excellence, which was developed by the U.S. Health Resources and Services Administration (HRSA). The primary goal of this nationwide program is to help medical schools increase their support of educational programs aimed at Hispanic students. The effort begins at the elementary school level by establishing, strengthening, and expanding programs to enhance the academic performance of students interested in attending medical school. In addition, the Hispanic Centers of Excellence target the pipeline in the colleges of medicine by supporting more Hispanic role models within the faculty ranks of the colleges of medicine. Finally, they carry out activities to improve the information resources, clinical education, curricula, and **cultural competence** of medical school graduates as they relate to minority health issues. With the exception of Colorado, there are Hispanic Centers of Excellence throughout the Southwest that target Mexican American students.[19]

■ Concluding Thoughts

A number of issues affect the access to health care of the Mexican-origin population in the United States. Foremost is the problem of financial access to health care. Clearly, this is tied to occupational location, which determines the income level of this subpopulation and whether or not they have access to private or publicly subsidized health insurance coverage. However, certain segments of the Mexican-origin population are more severely constrained by financial access issues than others. For example, senior citizens, undocumented immigrants, and women have special situations that interfere with their ability to effectively use both public and private health insurance.

Furthermore, the complexity of the U.S. health care financing system, which elevates private health insurance above universal coverage for all individuals, creates a policy dilemma for those of Mexican origin. Because most of this population falls within the category of the working poor, there is a need for targeted insurance programs in the non-unionized and small-business sectors, which are important employment sectors for the Mexican-origin population. Unless a serious attempt is made to address this gap between the voluntary health insurance market and the public sector, the uninsured rate for this population will continue to increase. Thus, the dilemma of financial health care access will continue until a coordinated effort is made to address the needs of this disproportionately uninsured group.

A final important point with regard to access is the shortage of Mexican-origin health care professionals to serve this population. As illustrated by the case of Mexican American physicians, the persistence of low numbers of medical applicants and graduates will continue without aggressive outreach efforts and early educational intervention. An excellent model for addressing this educational issue is provided by HRSA's program known as the Hispanic Centers of Excellence. This program combines early educational intervention in kindergarten through grade twelve with specific programming activities in the undergraduate and medical college experience of Hispanic students. In light of the attacks against affirmative action in the 1990s, structural models like the Hispanic Centers of Excellence will play a key role in ultimately meeting the AAMC's goal of increasing the percentage of minority medical students, including Mexican Americans, to parity (equivalence) with the overall U.S. population.

■ Discussion Exercises

1. What problems does the Mexican-origin community face in regard to financial access to health insurance?

2. What are the differences between publicly subsidized and private health insurance programs?

3. How does the lack of health insurance coverage affect the health status of the Mexican American population?

4. How does immigrant status affect the ability to obtain health care and insurance in the United States? Discuss in particular the difficulty of enrolling in public health insurance programs.

5. What is the relationship between occupational location and financial access to adequate health care services?

6. Why is it important to have parity in terms of minority health care professionals? What role does the education system play in reaching parity and increasing the pool of minority health care professionals?

■ Suggested Readings

Glaser, W. A. *Health Insurance in Practice.* San Francisco and Oxford: Jossey-Bass, 1991.

Hernández, D. J. *Children of Immigrants: Health, Adjustment, and Public Assistance.* Washington, D.C.: National Academy Press, 1999.

Kass, B. L., R. M. Weinick, and A. C. Monheit. *Racial and Ethnic Differences in Health, 1996.* MEPS Chartbook No. 2. Available from the Agency for Health Care Policy Research web site: www.meps.ahcpr.gov/papers/chartbk2/chartbk2a.htm

Medicare web site: www.medicare.gov

U.S. Bureau of the Census. *Health Insurance Coverage, 1997.* Current Population Reports, Series P60-202. Washington, D.C.: U.S. Bureau of the Census, September 1998.

Williams, S. J., and P. R. Torrens. *Introduction for Health Services.* 2d ed. New York: Wiley, 1984.

■ Notes

1. AHCCCS, the Arizona Health Care Cost Containment System, is the Arizona Medicaid-funded health program for the medically indigent.

2. S. J. Williams and P. R. Torrens, *Introduction to Health Services,* 2d ed. (New York: Wiley, 1984), p. 420.

3. J. Park and J. S. Buechner, "Race, Ethnicity, and Access to Health Care, Rhode Island," *Journal of Health and Social Policy* 9, no. 1 (1997).

4. U.S. Bureau of the Census, *Health Insurance Coverage: 1997,* Current Population

Reports Series P60-202 (Washington, D.C.: Government Printing Office, September 1998).

5. B. L. Kass, R. M. Weinick, and A. C. Monheit, *Racial and Ethnic Differences in Health 1996,* MEPS Chartbook No. 2, Agency for Health Care Policy Research; available from http://www.meps.ahcpr.gov/papers/chartbk2/chartbk2a.htm.

6. Social Security Administration web site: http://www.ssa.gov/search97cgi, search keyword SSI.

7. *Medicaid,* p. 1; available from the Health Care Financing Administration web site: http://www.hcfa.gov/medicaid/medicaid.htm.

8. Ibid., p. 4.

9. "What Is Medicare?" available from the Medicare web site: http://www.medicare.gov/whatis.html.

10. Ibid.

11. J. Guyer and C. Mann, "Employed but Not Insured: A State-by-State Analysis of the Number of Low-Income Working Parents Who Lack Health Insurance," p. 3; available from the Center on Budget and Policy Priorities web site: http://www.cbpp.org/2-9-99mcaid.htm.

12. "Heart disease, diabetes and cancer of the breast, colon, and cervix are the leading causes of death for Latinas living in the United States (14). These diseases are most likely to impact these women in their middle to elderly years. . . . For example, Mexican-born women represent 48 percent of all cancer deaths in the state of Texas and have 37 percent higher 28-day myocardial infarction mortality rates when compared to non-Latino white counterparts" (pp. 16, 17). "Other research has shown that Mexican women in the Southwest have two times the rate of cervical cancer than that of their non-Latino counterparts, which could be linked to the fact that a higher percentage of these women speak predominantly Spanish." (p. 19) "Also, less acculturated women over 50 years of age were much less likely to have had a mammogram" (p. 20). A. de la Torre, R. Friis, H. R. Hunter, B. K. Ellis, and L. García, "The Health Insurance Status of Latinas: A Population at Risk," *Journal of Border Health* [El Paso, Tex.] 4 (1999), 1–24.

13. A. de la Torre, R. Friis, H. R. Hunter, and L. García, "The Health Insurance Status of U.S. Latino Women: A Profile from the 1982–84 Hispanic HHANES," *American Journal of Public Health* 86, no. 4 (April 1996), p. 534.

14. This information is for August 1999. The Mexican minimum wage may be higher depending on geographical region. Instituto Nacional de Estadística, Geografía, e Informática web site: www.inegi.gob.mx/economia/español/feconomia.html.

15. Although the study from which this information was taken uses the term "Latino," the vast majority of the population under study were of Mexican origin; C. L. Schu, M. L. Burc, C. D. Good, and E. N. Gardner, *California's Undocumented*

Latino Immigrants: A Report on Access to Health Care Services (Bethesda, Md.: The Project HOPE Center for Health Affairs, 1999), p. 35.

16. D. L. Libby, Z. Zhou, and D. A. Kindig, "Will Minority Physician Supply Meet U.S. Needs?" *Health Affairs* 16, no. 4 (1997)

17. Association of American Medical Colleges (AAMC) *Project 3000 by 2000 Progress to Date: Year Four Progress Report* (Washington D.C.: AAMC, Division of Community and Minority Programs, 1996), p. 1.

18. Presentation by Jordon Cohen, M.D., president of the AAMC at the AAMC Conference, Washington, D.C., October 1999. In 1997, 796 Mexican Americans applied to medical schools in the United States. Approximately half of these were accepted and enrolled. However, since 1991, the number of Mexican American medical school applicants has decreased by almost 14 percent. This decline is directly related to the cutbacks in affirmative action programs in California and Texas, where a large number of Mexican-origin students reside.

19. HRSA, Division of Disadvantaged Assistance, Centers of Excellence web site: http://www.hrsa.dhhs.gov/bhpr/dda/coefact.htm.

5

"My doctor doesn't care"

CULTURAL COMPETENCY IN HEALTH CARE SERVICES

I t's like there's a clash there somewhere, and I don't know if it's cultural or what it is. I don't know if doctors understand how to deal with people who don't speak the language or Mexicans from Mexico or **Chicanos** or **Chicanas**. I don't know if there's a cultural clash or what it is exactly, but they tend to be a bit brisk at times or they shun people off like, "shut up." . . . (Marco G., 28)

Marco illustrates the frustration of many **Mexican Americans** who feel that they are not being provided with culturally competent health care. This frustration may be a result of the lack of health care professionals with Spanish language skills, health care professionals' perception that the patient uses negative stereotypes when addressing them in a clinical setting, or the general lack of cultural sensitivity in the diagnosis or treatment of an illness. This chapter will focus on the importance of both **linguistic** and **cultural competency** in providing quality health care to the Mexican-origin population. Given the introductory nature of this book, we will highlight the current issues and debates surrounding this topic. However, we recognize that this is a new and rapidly emerging field. There has been little analysis of the impact of linguistic and cultural competency on health care outcomes for the Mexican-origin population. Nevertheless, the voices of both patients and minority health care professionals have pushed this issue to the forefront of the national health care debate.

Linguistic Competency: A Significant Component of Cultural Competency

It was important to my mother that her doctor was Mexican or **Latino**. To her it made a difference because I can remember being seven or eight years old and translating what the doctor was saying. At the time I didn't think it was a big deal, but now that I look back I think that it was kind of hard on me because I felt that I had to clearly state what he was saying to her and vice versa. I don't know how well of a job I did at that time. That's why it was important to her to make sure that she had a doctor that could speak Spanish, that was **bilingual**. (Ana M., 26)

Ana, like many children of Mexican **immigrants**, experienced firsthand the dilemma of translating for her parents during visits to the doctor's office. In the absence of bilingual medical staff or an adult interpreter she was the only means of communication between her mother and the clinician. Ana's childhood experiences illustrate the frustrations and fears many children from Mexican immigrant families experience in translating for their parents when health problems that require direct medical intervention arise.

Unfortunately, many children of Mexican immigrants are still placed in the awkward position of seeking the best medical treatment for their family by acting as a linguistic bridge to the dominant culture and language of the United States. Yet given the sophistication of medical information, few children are able to effectively understand and synthesize it, which can result in potentially dangerous miscommunication between physician and patient. Therein lies the inherent weakness in relying on these young bridges to meet the linguistic needs of this large Spanish-speaking community. In states such as California that have large Hispanic populations, the need to provide linguistically competent health care to Spanish-speaking immigrants has become a major force in restructuring how health care is delivered. The goals are to minimize the need for family members to act as interpreters for relatives in the delivery of health care services and to increase the delivery of information through either professional interpreters on site or trained bilingual health care professionals.

Linguistic competency is critical to making **health care access** available to many Mexican immigrants. Linguistic competency, for most health care professionals, is defined as the availability of health care information and services in the language of the patient. The key is whether health care professionals can communicate with Spanish-speaking clients in a way that results in improved health outcomes for the clients and lower costs for the providers of these services. As recent Mexican immigrants become the dominant segment of the Mexican-origin population, the need for bilingual health professionals will increase.

Newly arrived immigrants generally have little education, do not speak English, and are less acculturated. Therefore, they are at greater risk of encountering barriers to health care when they are not provided with linguistically competent health care providers.[1] Monolingual Spanish speakers are also at the greatest risk of not obtaining health care because of their lower rate of private health insurance coverage compared to bilingual Spanish-English and monolingual English speakers.[2] Thus, language plays an important role in allowing recent Mexican immigrants to access health care in the United States.

Linguistic competency is an essential component of cultural competency for the Mexican-origin population given its demographic profile and recent immigrant status. California's model for contracting managed care plans for the more than three million Medi-Cal (California's state **Medicaid** program) beneficiaries has been relatively successful in addressing the linguistic competency issue. In order to address the state's multicultural health care needs, it was determined that linguistic needs of non-English-speaking health plan members must be met. Therefore, California requires that health plans contracting to serve the Medi-Cal-eligible population must translate health plan materials into the language of non-English-speaking clients and have access to twenty-four-hour interpreter services. A lesson learned from the California experience is that the first step to meeting cultural needs for immigrant populations is through the introduction of linguistic services within the health care system.[3]

Beyond the issue of translation and interpreter services within health care settings is the profile of the medical staff at the site. The California experience also highlights the need for incentives to hire more **Hispanic** and Mexican-origin physicians within the Medi-Cal delivery system. As many of these providers share both language and similar cultural values with the patients they serve, they are better equipped to understand the cultural nuances of the largely monolingual and bilingual Mexican- origin population. Unfortunately, the paucity of Hispanic physicians in the United States has resulted in a significant shortage of bilingual, culturally competent health care providers. As discussed in chapter 4, the prospects of meeting the growing demand for bilingual and **bicultural** doctors in the near future appears bleak. As illustrated in table 5.1, Mexican-origin students comprised only 2.2 percent of the total medical school graduates in 1996–1997.

Focusing solely on Spanish language competency as the defining characteristic of linguistic competency is problematic, however. Since language is

Table 5.1 Ethnic Backgrounds of 1997 Medical School Graduates

ETHNIC BACKGROUND	PERCENTAGE
African American	7.5
Native American/Alaskan Native	0.6
Mexican American	2.2
Puerto Rican[1]	1.9
Other Hispanic	1.9
Asian/Pacific Islander	15.5
All other students[2]	70.4

1. Includes Commonwealth and mainland students.
2. Includes white students and international students of various ethnic backgrounds.
Source: American Medical Association web site: www.ama-assn.org/mem-data/mimed/table6.htm.

symbolic of the broader cultural experience of Mexican Americans and Mexican immigrants, understanding the cultural nuances and idiosyncratic belief structure of this group is critical to interpreting language. Thus, a broader definition of competency should include an understanding of Mexican folklore and health.

 ## The Impact of Mexican Folklore, Language, and Health

> The only times that we ended up in the hospital or in the doctor's office is when it was an extreme emergency. All other things, such as the upset stomachs, the burns, the cuts, the scrapes, were taken care of by herbs, teas, and home remedies, which my mother had great knowledge of. She was very well versed in the folkloric healing caused by, for example, el **mal de ojo**, **susto**, and **empacho**. (Gracie S., 46)

Gracie illustrates how low-income immigrant families often rely on a family member to provide treatment for childhood and family illnesses. In many Mexican immigrant families, the health care providers are mothers who learned of Mexican folklore illnesses and remedies through their kinship ties. This is further illustrated by Gracie's childhood experience with the mumps:

> We ended up getting mumps all at the same time. There were nine of us and seven of us ended up with the mumps. This was a struggle

for my mother because we all had high fevers. She didn't have money for pain medication or fever medication; she just knew how to do things according to how she was raised. She knew that the discomfort of mumps was alleviated by applying heat, so she sauteed tomatoes and wrapped them around our cheeks. And she would saute tomatoes and put them on the bottom of our feet. (Gracie S., 46)

Gracie's family experience with the mumps illustrates why a clinician would need to have not only command of the Spanish language, but also some familiarity with cultural interpretations of illnesses and traditional treatments used by Mexican immigrants. Oftentimes linguistic competency is viewed solely as the ability of a clinician to speak to patients in their native language as well as in English. However, linguistic competency must go beyond translation by bilingual medical personnel. It must include health promotion and educational materials that are culturally appropriate and at the literacy level of the patient. Given the low educational levels of many Mexican immigrants, linguistically appropriate material needs to use suitable media of communication so that patients fully understand treatments for themselves and their families. This may require medical providers to be sensitive to regional dialects of Spanish as well as the use and knowledge of idiomatic expressions and cultural beliefs of diseases, which convey certain health disorders. Many of these illnesses are rooted in the spiritual and folkloric domains of Mexican culture and may be expressed by Mexican immigrants as actual diseases. Emotional and physiological responses to these perceived illnesses can be understood only if the health provider is both linguistically and culturally aware of these beliefs. According to Margarita Kay:

Many health problems have names that are readily recognizable across cultures. In the American and Mexican West, however, some of these illnesses have old-fashioned names that were once the established terms for specific diseases but which are seen today simply as symptoms by biomedicine ("Fever" is one example). . . . Folk illnesses, called "Mexican diseases" by Mexican Americans because "American doctors don't believe in them," have other seemingly obsolete names.[4]

Table 5.2 lists symptomatic diseases that do not have exact English translations or counterparts, illustrating the cultural and idiomatic speci-

Table 5.2 Some Common Folkloric Diseases and Their Treatments

DISEASE	DEFINITION	TREATMENT
Empacho	Swollen belly resulting from massage by a sobadora, or undigested food causing gastrointestinal distress.	Drinking herbal teas such as yerba buena (peppermint) or manzanilla (chamomile).
Espanto	Susto or fright caused by seeing a ghost or by being awakened suddenly; more serious than susto.	Retrieving one's soul, limpia, or house blessing.
Mal de ojo	Often mistranslated as "the evil eye," a correct translation is "illness caused by staring"; results when infants or children receive more attention than usual; can result in restlessness, vomiting, or fever.	Rubbing an egg over the child as prayers are recited using a special charm or amulet.
Mollera caída	In infants this represents a fallen fontanel, which may be a result of dehydration.	Wetting the baby's head with warm water, soaping the soft spot, then gently pushing up on the palate while pulling the hairs at the soft spot.
Pasmo	Swellings and skin eruptions resulting from rapid chilling of the body following excessive activity or bleeding.	N/A
Pujos	In infants, grunting or straining as a result of contact with menstruating women or persons who have recently had sexual intercourse.	N/A

Sources: E. Ávila and J. Parker, *Woman Who Glows in the Dark* (New York: Jeremy P. Tarcher/ Putnam, 1999); R. T. Trotter and J. A. Chavira, *Curanderismo, Mexican American Folk Healing.* (Athens, Ga.: University of Georgia Press, 1997).

ficity of Mexican diseases. Such folklore illnesses are embedded in cultural interpretations that may result in patient-clinician misunderstanding if the medical staff is unaware of them. The situation is further complicated when a patient treats an illness with folklore remedies. Within the cultural parameters of Mexican folklore are herbal remedies used for treatment of a disease, as illustrated in table 5.2. **Curanderas/os** (folk healers) use many treatments, both medicinal and ritual, to help people recover from the illnesses listed in the table and others. Two common treatments are *limpias* (literally, "cleanings") and *pláticas* ("conversations" or "chats"). Limpia is a spiritual cleansing used to heal emotional trauma that may or may not be manifesting itself physically. This treatment often involves the sweeping of an egg or bundles of herbs over the body to "cleanse a person's energy." This may be done in combination with praying or chanting. Elena Ávila, a Mexican American curandera, calls pláticas "heart-to-heart talks" that basically perform the functions of culturally sensitive counseling. Pláticas help the curandera and patient to discover together the possible causes of an illness, and can be curative in themselves. These two types of treatment are used, in various forms, to treat a range of emotional/spiritual and physical illnesses. Because of a lack of health insurance, it is not uncommon for Mexican-origin persons, especially low-income immigrants, to seek alternative treatments or delay treatment for a disease until a medical crisis emerges.[5]

Anthropologists have conducted much of the research on Mexican folklore illnesses and treatment, and there is very little documentation of the extent of folklore practices within the Mexican-origin community. Again, a lack of financial access to health care may lead to greater reliance on kinship ties to diagnose and treat the symptoms of an illness. Although the documented evidence to date provides little support for widespread use of traditional Mexican healers (including curanderas, **parteras**, or **sobadoras**), knowledgeable family members may often act as substitutes for these healers.

Recent health care literature is instructive on how cultural competency can be integrated into the health care delivery system. This literature further develops the idea of incorporating individual cultural beliefs and practices as mediating factors in diagnosing and treating patients. This broader definition provides an opportunity for improving access to and quality of health care for the Mexican-origin population.

 ## Cultural Competency: Implications for the Mexican-Origin Population

Cultural Competency is a process that requires individuals and systems to develop and expand their ability to know about, be sensitive to, and have respect for cultural diversity. The result of this process should be an increased awareness, acceptance, valuing, and utilization of and an openness to learn from general and health-related beliefs, practices, traditions, languages, religions, histories, and current needs of individuals and the cultural groups to which they belong. Essential to cultural competency is appropriate and effective communication. This requires the willingness to listen and learn from members of diverse cultures and the provision of services and information in appropriate languages, at appropriate comprehension and literacy levels, and in the context of individuals' cultural health beliefs and practices.[6]

During the last decade the body of literature focusing on cultural competency and access to quality health care has increased. As the nation's minority population continues to grow, the lack of minority trained health professionals and general ignorance of cultural issues will continue to create health care access barriers for this population. Given the individual health care risks and the health care system costs associated with limited access, cultural competency has moved from the margins of the health care debates to the forefront.

In the area of substance abuse prevention there is a significant body of literature describing interventions that are sensitive to ethnic, racial, gender, regional, and class differences within targeted populations. A significant amount of this work has focused on the Hispanic community in general without examining inter- and intra-group differences, limiting its usefulness for the Mexican-origin population. However, research suggests that health care providers who have a clear understanding of differences between Hispanic groups will be more effective in developing cost-effective programs for them.

Another rich source of information is the literature on mental health. Yet, despite the significance of this work in isolating unique cultural behaviors of distinct Hispanic **subpopulations**, this literature often ignores the historical experience of immigrants. Without an understanding of how Mexican immigrants enter the United States and acculturate, only a superficial understanding of their culture is possible. For many Mexican immigrants, the way they enter the United States influences how they construct their identity and minority group status. This is illustrated by the following interview with Martín:

> I came here when I was nine. . . . My mother was back in Mexico. After my grandmother died I felt like I didn't belong there [in

Mexico] anymore so I wanted to get away and I was sent over [to live] with my aunt in the United States. I was closer to my grandmother than I was to my mother. . . . In the beginning it was tough because there was a language barrier. I didn't know how to speak a word of English and there was no bilingual program. I had a cousin who had the same classes and translated what was going on in the classroom for me, but it was hard to pick up the language. All of the kids made fun of you and called you wetback and *mojado* because you couldn't speak the language and they knew you were from a different country. So it was hard. (Martín G., 31)

Martín illustrates the ambivalent feelings that Mexican immigrants often have about living in the United States. Even though his "push factors" (reasons for leaving Mexico) were personal, related to the loss of his beloved grandmother, his reception into the United States was less than hospitable. His ethnic identity and his limited English skills caused him to suffer the discrimination that many Mexican immigrants have experienced in the Southwest. Thus, his identity has been shaped by his ethnicity and the discrimination he has faced. Unfortunately, the literature on public health glosses over this social construction of ethnic identity and the multiple dimensions of cultural and individual identity.

Martín's case also illustrates another important factor in framing culturally competent interventions, which is recognizing the immigrant status of the Mexican-origin population. Immigrant status affects not only language preference (level of Spanish or English proficiency), but also the relative importance of cultural practices from Mexico. For example, much of the literature that focuses on positive birth outcomes (for example, low infant **mortality**) analyzes data of recent Mexican immigrant women. Studies by David Hayes Bautista and colleagues illustrate well the differences between Mexican immigrant women and Mexican Americans of later generations.[7] Generally, immigrant women are likely to adhere to more rigid class and male-female cultural norms, including those relating to health care issues such as the use of traditional home remedies to self-treat an ailment or condition.

As children of immigrants become acculturated through both their new educational and social milieus, perceptions and health care practices begin to change. Moreover, particularly for young Mexican American women there is significant historical evidence of increased intergenerational conflict as young women develop a new sense of social identity and placement within the larger society. This legacy of intergenerational conflict is best illustrated in Vicki Ruiz' analysis of Mexican-origin women in Los Angeles in the 1930s. Conflicts erupted within families as young **Latinas** attempted to emulate the Hollywood standard of the day in behavior and dress:

> Within families, young women, perhaps more than their brothers, were expected to uphold certain standards. Indeed, Chicano/a social scientists have generally portrayed women as "the 'glue' that keeps the Chicano family together" and as the guardians of "traditional culture." Parents, therefore, often assumed what they perceived as their unquestionable prerogative to regulate the actions and attitudes of their adolescent daughters. Teenagers, on the other hand, did not always acquiesce in the boundaries set down for them by their elders. Intergenerational tension flared along several fronts.[8]

In many respects, children of immigrants create blended or bicultural identities that may challenge traditional roles while symbolically still supporting traditional markers of ethnic identity such as language and religious practices. Biculturalism within immigrant and ethnic groups is not unique to the Mexican-origin population. Dual identity and cultural practices are seen in most Latino/a groups, including Dominicans, Puerto Ricans, and Cubans.[9] Understanding the cultural identity of Mexican Americans and other Hispanic subgroups is a first step in appropriately defining culturally specific health care practices and interventions.

 ## Understanding the Role of Gender and Cultural Competency

> I'm a wife, mother, a grandmother and as you probably already know in the Latin families the mother is the pillar of the house so if I'm sick everybody's sick. The most important thing is that you keep yourself together so that your family won't fall apart, because in Latin families the mother is supposed to be the pillar so it's very hard when you're sick. I'm very lucky and blessed that my family backs me up. When I'm going downhill they'll push me back up, and that's one of the best and most important things in a Latin family is that we're tight and we're together. (Yolanda N., 52)

Yolanda's perception of gender roles is a critical component of understanding her cultural identity. In many instances both men and women may project culturally appropriate behavioral practices, but in reality renegotiate these roles within their daily life activities. One of the major problems in training programs that focus on cultural competency is that they generalize and refer to cultural stereotypes when describing accepted gender roles.[10] Instead of conforming to a monolithic ideal of gendered behavior, it seems that most Mexican-origin women, including Mexican immigrant women, question or shift boundaries, particularly as they renegotiate their gender roles with increased **acculturation**, which in turn affects health behaviors.[11] Mexican-origin women define their gender roles within their culture, which will determine how receptive they may be to frank discussions on, for example, sexuality, alcohol use, or child-rearing practices. Therefore, the intersection of gender, cultural identity, and culture for Mexican American women must be understood *before* a model of culturally competent health care can be developed for these women.

Mexican immigrant and Mexican American women have largely been defined by cultural behavioral norms that describe gender relations. The terms most commonly used to describe these interactions between men and women are **marianismo, malinchismo, machismo,** and **familismo.** These terms, however, have also been used to describe the Mexican-origin population in the United States who have not assimilated into mainstream culture.

Mexican-origin and other Latina women have often been described in terms of marianismo. In *The Maria Paradox,* marianismo is defined as "the ideal role of woman . . . taking as its model of perfection the Virgin Mary herself. Marianismo is about sacred duty, self-sacrifice, and chastity. About dispensing care and pleasure, not receiving them. About living in the shadows, literally and figuratively, of your men—father, boyfriend, husband, son—your kids, and your family."[12]

Many researchers have relied on this definition without understanding the complexity of these gender stereotypes, which has resulted in a superficial description of the behavior of Mexican-origin women who reside in the United States. However, Chicana scholars view these behavioral characteristics specifically through the lens of Mexican American culture. These scholars have analyzed these behaviors in the context of the historical experiences of Mexican Americans who participated in the Chicano movement (Mexican American civil rights movement) that emerged during the 1960s. For example, citing Rendon, Angie Chabram Dernersesian explains machismo in the following manner: "The essence of machismo, of being macho, is as much a symbolic principle for the Chicano revolt as it is a guideline for family life. . . . Macho, in other words, can no longer relate merely to manhood but must relate to nationhood as well. . . . The word Chicano in many ways embodies the revolt itself."[13]

Within the context of the work of Chicana scholars, terms such as machismo, marianismo, and familismo have deeper symbolic definitions that include resistance to the dominant culture as a reaction to the historical legacy of racial discrimination in the Southwest. Moreover, Chicana feminist scholars have analyzed how Chicana/Mexican American women have resisted the negative characterization associated with ethnic and gender stereotypes. These scholars have redefined the negative connotations of many of these behavioral characteristics. This is clearly illustrated by the reconstruction of the term malinchismo, which once symbolized betrayal of one's own culture and people, into a meaning of resistance and strength.[14]

While gender stereotypes are sometimes reaffirmed in Mexican women's attitudes and behavior, recent works in Chicana scholarship indicate that even immigrant women question the validity of these stereotypical roles by redefining them. This literature shows a clear pattern of Mexican-origin men and women renegotiating their traditional roles as their levels of economic participation and exposure to a new social milieu alter over time. Beatríz Pesquera illustrates this pattern in her research on the division of household labor within Mexican-origin families. In Pesquera's study, traditional gender roles in Mexican-origin families were altered by the women's economic contributions to household incomes.[15]

 ## Implementation of Cultural Competency: Implications for the Mexican-Origin Population

I think that health care providers need to start thinking outside the box, look at our communities and really go towards directing the information to where it is needed. . . . I feel that the Anglo population has a wealth of information directed to its community about exercise, about nutrition. They have exercise programs, self-help books, and so forth. They have all sorts of information, and yet that information is not reaching our communities. I don't think it is

> reaching the masses. . . . In terms of prevention, nutrition, diet, and the need to exercise, that message needs to be there. (Gracie S., 46)

To date there is little empirical evidence linking health care outcomes with varying levels of cultural competency of providers. Nonetheless, the goal of cultural competency is to enhance communication skills so individuals of different ethnic backgrounds will have greater access to cost-effective and high-quality health care, including preventive care information. However, as illustrated previously, the theoretical and empirical base that is used for Mexican immigrants and Mexican Americans must be further developed.

The implementation of cultural competency in a health care setting may be divided into the following three domains:

1. Acculturation models focused on developing descriptions of minority populations to assist in targeting culturally appropriate medical interventions
2. Specific models for therapeutic treatment of identified minority groups
3. **Process evaluation** models aimed at changing the organizational climate of the health plan or site

These models are briefly summarized in the following sections.

Acculturation Models

> I think it's important for the overall Hispanic community, whether you are Mexican, Cuban, or Puerto Rican, to learn more about the laws of the United States. And I think it is important for them to understand and get a grasp of the language. I know maybe some people don't want to learn the language, but they should at least know how to communicate with the rest of the world around them. (Martín G., 31)

Research on Hispanic acculturation is extensive in both the mental health and public health literatures. The importance of this research in explaining health behaviors and the **health status** of Hispanics, particularly Mexican Americans and Mexican immigrants, cannot be overstated. For example, the acculturation scale developed by Cuellar, Harris, and Jasso is used frequently to assess the levels to which immigrant Hispanics, particularly those of Mexican origin, are relatively less or more acculturated into mainstream American society. Although the Cuellar scale has a number of **variables** related to levels of ethnic interaction as well as family and self-identification, the most significant variable is the level of English language acquisition vis-à-vis the level of native language retention.[16] Thus, it is not surprising that level of English language proficiency becomes a critical factor in defining acculturation levels of Hispanics. The pressure on immigrants who lack English proficiency to achieve economic success creates enormous psychological pressure resulting in further ethnic isolation. According to Padilla and Salgado, "in the general literature on cross-cultural mental health, migration in and of itself is identified as a source of stress for the individual. . . . The immigrant is at high risk for experiencing severe bouts of psychosocial conflict because of self-imposed pressure to succeed and the lack of English proficiency."[17] Acculturation models predict that English language acquisition and proficiency will determine how well Hispanic immigrants assimilate into the dominant culture, which in turn affects their ability to access health care and health care information.

Therapeutic Treatment Models

There is a large body of literature specific to therapeutic treatment that helps mental health professionals assess the external issues that may frame the behavior of minority individuals who have experienced racism. These models are not specific to the Mexican-origin population but provide some insight into the effects of discrimination on the psychosocial responses of minority clients. Thus, they provide a therapeutic framework for clinicians to treat patients suffering from depression or other psychological disorders. For example, in their work Sue and Sue identify a common thread among all oppressed groups, which is represented in the framework of observed attitudes toward the dominant group.[18] This linear stage model uses a cultural framework to understand levels of ethnic identity formation. It enables the therapist to assess where a minority individual may "fit" within the process of identity formation. According to Sue and Sue, individuals in the early stage are completely dominated by the majority group. Therefore, they exhibit a strong tendency to assimilate into the broader society and devalue their own ethnic culture relative to this dominant culture. By stage three, characteristics of resistance emerge within minority individuals resulting in the absolute denial of the validity of the dominant culture. A self-immersion within one's ethnic culture may also occur. Finally, by stage 5, the last stage, integrative awareness, the individual has resolved previous conflicts with the dominant society and has established his/her own identity and sense of security.[19] Cultural competency within this framework focuses on deviations from the dominant culture and identifies the extent to which a minority individual attempts to integrate into and adopt the dominant culture. These therapeutic models help to categorize observed attitudes and behaviors of minority individuals that may mediate their mental health problems.

These types of frameworks predict minority behavior in relation to the dominant culture and suggest treatment strategies based on the degree to which the individual exhibits specific levels of minority-majority integration. This model may be helpful in a clinical setting for treating specific mental health disorders. On the other hand, it may underestimate the degree to which Mexican Americans and Mexican immigrants **code switch** both language and behavior based on a given social setting. Code switching may occur, for example, when a Mexican American patient uses idiomatic expressions and behaviors with a Mexican-origin clinician but not with a non-Mexican clinician, based on an implicit assumption of cultural understanding between the two individuals. Given this implicit assumption, the patient's behavior with a non-ethnically matched health care professional may be more guarded. In addition, the patient may attempt to adopt language and behavior that is more culturally attuned to the clinician's culture rather than relying on his or her preferred cultural behavioral norms for communication.

Therapeutic models that consider cultural competency are important to develop. However, a great deal more research is needed to assess their **efficacy in treatment** for the Mexican-origin population. Consideration of changes in cultural behavior based on the health care environment and ethnicity of the clinician should be built into any therapeutic model used in the treatment of Mexican-origin patients.

Models of Organizational Climate

Most of the more general literature on cultural competency focuses on the organizational climate and individual behaviors of providers in specific health care settings. Categories of acculturation may be defined with respect to language or specific cultural practices using an inventory model approach. To date, little research has focused on measuring outcomes of

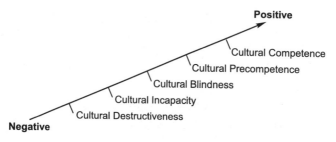

Figure 13. Continuum of Cultural Competence

cultural interventions used in therapeutic treatment. Even though the body of literature on acculturation and therapeutic treatment suggests the importance of culturally competent care, there is a dearth of clinical outcome data. Nonetheless, cultural competency training of medical staff is well underway in many health care organizations across the country. Cultural competency programs used for training purposes combine self-examination and criticism of provider bias using specific models that place an individual's behavior within a continuum of attitudes and behaviors (see figure 13).[20]

Assuming that a continuum of organizational behavior, ranging from culturally destructive to culturally competent, exists within health care settings, a plan for training can be developed within these parameters. Ultimately, the goal of the multicultural or sensitivity training curriculum is for providers to become more empathetic to the needs of minority and ethnic groups by modifying the culturally destructive and culturally blind behaviors.[21]

 ## A Patient's Guide for Assessing the Cultural Competency of a Health Care Provider

How would you assess whether your health care provider is culturally sensitive or culturally or linguistically competent? One way to ensure culturally and linguistically competent health care is to obtain good information about the health care providers you are interested in or have access to. Asking friends or relatives for recommendations of Spanish-speaking or culturally sensitive health care providers is one such strategy. Remember that it is important to ask questions regarding your health. The following are some guidelines to consider in choosing physicians, nurses, and other health care providers who are linguistically and culturally competent:

1. Is the health care provider of Mexican origin, Hispanic, or a member of another minority group?
2. Does the health care provider share your cultural values?
3. Is the health care provider located in your community?
4. Does the practitioner provide bilingual or interpreter services? Is the practitioner or medical staff bilingual? Can the interpreter provide adequate and accurate medical translations?
5. How well does the health care provider listen to you? Does the person answer or dismiss your questions? Do you feel the person cares about and respects you?
6. Do you feel the health care provider advocates for your health interests? Do you have to struggle with the practitioner when you need specialist referrals or specific medications?
7. Does the practitioner provide written materials in languages other than English?
8. Does the practitioner provide other resources and references that are linguistically and/or culturally sensitive?
9. Does the clinic provide convenient times for scheduling appointments and appointment times that accommodate your work and family schedule? Are there barriers to flexible access in terms of scheduling your medical appointments (which may include non-culturally or linguistically sensitive staff)?[22]

 **Beyond Cultural Competency:
Some Final Thoughts**

I really truly believe my doctor doesn't care about me because I'm Mexican. When I got the consultation I saw that 90 percent of his patients are Americans, white, and I'm Mexican American. I really believe that because my doctor took two months to do a blood test. It doesn't make sense. I've been calling and everything and all they say is tomorrow, tomorrow. So I really feel discriminated on that part and I don't feel good about it. (Yolanda N., 52)

A major problem not addressed in the research is the underlying assumption that cultural competency training of medical staff is sufficient to enable clinicians and health care professionals to provide quality health care to culturally or linguistically distinct minority groups. In general, one must accept the proposition that any individual can be trained to become "bicompetent"; that is, able to understand cultural and linguistic differences and evaluate information based on this knowledge. A fundamental problem with this premise is that unlike language, where one can measure specific skills in spoken, written, and reading proficiency, culture does not have a static domain in which one can measure specific skills. Moreover, the nature of culture as a process that individuals display when interacting with mainstream society is laden with ambiguity. As anthropologist Renato Rosaldo writes, "when in doubt, people find out about their worlds by living with ambiguity, uncertainty, or simple lack of knowledge . . . we often improvise, learn by doing, and make things up as we go along."[23] Therefore, although certain customs and practices may indicate an individual's specific cultural preference, they must be interpreted with the understanding that they may not reflect key cultural factors. Some behaviors may very well be signs of hybrid biculturalism rather than reflecting a degree of acculturation within the Mexican-origin community.

These issues pose important questions about our ability to develop models for measuring the cultural competence of health care strategies. Given the nuances of behavior and specific cultural characteristics of the Mexican-origin population, successful health care settings will be those that bridge the two cultures. The employment of Mexican-origin health care professionals will be a key part of that success. Moreover, the delicate balance between ferreting out cultural competency variables and providing a practical basis for assessing outcomes merits considerable attention and continued research. Both process and therapeutic variables must be clearly defined with measurable standards. However, we should be aware that how each of us defines culture and language is idiosyncratic and reflects our own life experiences. This is an important caveat for all health care professionals because it suggests that a learned-skills approach may not be sufficient to develop a culturally competent delivery system. If it is not, recruiting bicompetent health care providers from specific Hispanic subpopulations will be necessary.

■ Discussion Exercises

1. Distinguish between linguistic competency and cultural competency as it relates to the health care setting, including access to and receiving health care.

2. How would increasing the number of Mexican-origin medical staff (physicians, nurses, insurance personnel, health care administrators) improve access to adequate and culturally competent health care?

3. What role does cultural background play in health care issues for the Mexican-origin population?

4. How does an individual's ethnic identity (i.e., identifying as Mexican American, Chicano/a, or Hispanic), affect the manner in which a patient perceives his/her relationship with a health care provider and the health care setting?

5. Why is it important for a clinician or health care provider to understand the cultural differences that exist among various patients, particularly those of non-white ethnic backgrounds?

6. Distinguish between acculturation and biculturalism as it relates to the Mexican-origin population.

7. What is the biggest obstacle to implementing an optimal culturally competent health care setting?

■ Suggested Readings

Ávila, E., and J. Parker. *Woman Who Glows in the Dark*. New York: Jeremy P. Tarcher/Putnam, 1999.

Cross, T., B. Bazron, E. Dennis, and M. Isaacs. *Toward a Culturally Competent System of Care*. Vol. 1. Washington, D.C.: CASSP, Georgetown University, 1989.

Dean, R. G. "Understanding Health Beliefs and Behaviors: Some Theoretical Principles of Practice." In *Removing Cultural and Ethnic Barriers to Health Care*, pp. 49–67. Chapel Hill: University of North Carolina Press, 1979.

Desmond, J. "Communicating with Multicultural Patients." *Life in Medicine* (1994), pp. 7–25.

Harwood, A. "Ethnicity and Medical Care." Cambridge, Mass.: Harvard University Press, 1981.

Isaacs, M. R., and M. P. Benjamin. "Toward a Culturally Competent System of Care." In *Monographs of Programs Which Utilize Culturally Competent Principles*. Washington, D.C.: CASSP, Georgetown University, 1991.

Kay, M. *Healing with Plants*. Tucson: University of Arizona Press, 1996.

———. *Spanish-English, English-Spanish Medical Dictionary of the Southwest*. 2d. ed. Tucson: University of Arizona Press, 2001.

Lecca, P. L., I. Quervalú, J. V. Nunes, and H. F. Gonzales. *Cultural Competency in*

Health, Social, and Human Services. New York and London: Garland Publishing, 1998.

Office of Minority Health Resource Center web site, Cultural Competency Resources: http://www.omhrc.gov/clas/index.htm (linguistic) and http://www.omhrc.gov/New.HTM#cecp (cultural).

Pernell-Arnold, A. *Diversity and Health Care Training.* (Training curricula). Philadelphia: APAC, 1995.

Power, J. G., and T. Byrd. *U.S.-Mexico Border Health: Issues for Regional and Migrant Populations.* Thousand Oaks, Calif.: Sage Publications, 1998.

Pulido, L. *Environmentalism and Economic Justice: Two Chicano Struggles in the Southwest.* Tucson: University of Arizona Press, 1996.

Trotter, R. T. II, and J. A. Chavira, *Curanderismo: Mexican American Folk Healing.* 2d. ed. Athens, Ga.: University of Georgia Press, 1997.

U.S. Department of Health and Human Services. Surgeon General's National Hispanic/Latino Health Initiatives. *One Voice, One Vision—Recommendations to the Surgeon General to Improve Hispanic/Latino Health.* Washington, D.C.: Government Printing Office, 1993.

U.S. Department of Health and Human Services, Office of Minority Health, "Assuring Cultural Competence in Health Care: Recommendations for National Standards and an Outcomes-Focused Research Agenda: Recommendations for National Standards and a National Public Comment Process." Available from the Office of Minority Health web site: http://www.omhrc.gov/clas/index.htm.

■ Notes

1. A. L. Estrada, F. M. Treviño, and L. A. Ray, "Health Care Utilization Barriers among Mexican Americans: Evidence from HHANES 1982–84," *American Journal of Public Health* 80, suppl. (1990), p. 30.

2. C. L. Shur and L. A. Albers, "Language, Sociodemographics, and Health Care Use of Hispanic Adults," *Journal of Health Care for the Poor and Underserved* 7, no. 2 (1996).

3. M. Coye and D. Alvarez, *Medicaid Managed Care and Cultural Diversity in California* (San Francisco: The Lewin Group, The Commonwealth Fund, March 1999), p. v.

4. M. A. Kay, *Healing with Plants* (Tucson: University of Arizona Press, 1996), p. 52.

5. E. Ávila and J. Parker, *Woman Who Glows in the Dark* (New York: Jeremy P. Tarcher/Putnam, 1999); R. T. Trotter and J. A. Chavira, *Curanderismo, Mexican American Folk Healing* (Athens, Ga.: University of Georgia Press, 1997).

6. California Cultural Competency Task Force, *Recommendations for the Medi-Cal Managed Care Program* (Berkeley: Institute for the Study of Social Change, University of California, Berkeley, 1994), p. 1.

7. D. E. Hayes Bautista, W. O. Schink, and J. Chapa, *The Burden of Support: Young Latinos in an Aging Society* (Stanford: Stanford University Press, 1988), pp. 93–114.

8. V. L. Ruiz, "Star Struck," in *Building with Our Hands: New Directions in Chicana Studies,* eds. A. de la Torre and B. M. Pesquera, pp. 109–29 (Berkeley: University of California Press, 1993).

9. For more information on the construction of ethnic identity by other Latino/a groups, see L. E. Guarnizo, "Los Dominicanyorks: The Making of a Binational Society," in *Challenging Fronteras: Structuring Latina and Latino Lives in the United States,* eds. M. Romero, P. Hondagneu-Sotelo, and V. Ortiz, pp. 169–72 (New York: Routledge, 1997); J. Flores, "Qué Assimilated Brother, Yo Soy Asimilao: The Structuring of Puerto Rican Identity in the United States," in *Challenging Fronteras,* pp. 169–72; A. Portes and A. Stepick, "A Repeat Performance? The Nicaraguan Exodus," in *Challenging Fronteras,* p. 147; C. Nelson and M. Tienda, "The Structuring of Hispanic Ethnicity: Historical and Contemporary Perspectives," in *Challenging Fronteras,* p. 24.

10. A. de la Torre, "Hard Choices and Changing Roles among Mexican Migrant Campesinas," in *Building with Our Hands,* pp. 168–78.

11. D. A. Segura and A. de la Torre, "La Sufrida: Contradictions of Acculturation and Gender in Latina Health," in *Revisioning Women, Health, and Healing,* eds. A. E. Clarke and V. L. Oleson, pp. 155–63 (New York and London: Routledge, 1999).

12. R. M. Gil and C. I. Vazquez, *The Maria Paradox: How Latinas Can Merge Old World Traditions with New World Self-Esteem* (New York: The Berkeley Publishing Group, 1996), p. 7.

13. A. C. Dernersesian, "And Yes . . . The Earth Did Part," in *Building with Our Hands,* p. 163.

14. Ibid.

15. B. Pesquera, "In the Beginning He Wouldn't Lift a Spoon: The Division of Household Labor," in *Building with Our Hands,* pp. 181–95.

16. I. Cuellar, L. C. Harris, and R. Jasso, "An Acculturation Scale for Mexican American Normal and Clinical Populations," *Hispanic Journal of Behavioral Sciences* 2, no. 3, (1980), p. 208.

17. A. M. Padilla and V. N. Salgado de Snyder, "Hispanics: What the Culturally Informed Evaluator Needs to Know," in *Cultural Competence for Evaluators: A Guide for Alcohol and Other Drug Abuse Prevention Practitioners Working with Ethnic/Racial Communities,* eds. M. A. Orlandi, R. Weston, and L. G. Epstein, pp. 117–46 (Rockville, Md.: U.S. Department of Health and Human Services, Public Health Service, Alcohol, Drug Abuse, and Mental Health Administration, 1992).

18. D. W. Sue and D. Sue, *Counseling the Culturally Different* (New York: Independent Publishers Group–David White, 1990).

19. For a more complete discussion of the model presented by Sue and Sue, see

chapter 2 in P. J. Lecca, I. Quervalú, J. V. Nunes, and H. F. Gonzales, *Cultural Competency in Health, Social, and Human Services* (New York: Garland Publishing, 1998).

20. Lecca, Quervalú, Nunes, and Gonzales. *Cultural Competency in Health, Social, and Human Services,* pp. 51–54.

21. Ibid., pp. 52–54.

22. For more information on cultural competency, see Arizona Hispanic Center of Excellence, University of Arizona web site: http://www.hispanichealth.arizona.edu or The National Conference of State Legislatures Resources for Cross-Cultural Health Care Henry J. Kaiser Family Foundation. Diversity Rx at www.diversityRx.org.

23. R. Rosaldo, *Culture and Truth: The Remaking of Social Analysis* (Boston: Beacon Press, 1989), p. 152.

6

"This is about healing, about people getting better prevention"

FUTURE TRENDS IN MEXICAN AMERICAN HEALTH

There are many important issues to consider in assessing the health of the Mexican-origin population in the United States. The health of this group influences the overall data on Hispanic health, as Mexican-origin people make up the largest **Hispanic subpopulation**. Even though data are often combined under the broad category "Hispanic," it is necessary to differentiate between subgroups. For this reason, we have sought to outline key factors that influence the **health status** and access issues of **Mexican Americans**. With the continuing rapid growth of the Hispanic population, it is becoming increasingly important to have research that provides information specific to Hispanic subgroups. Such information is needed to develop more effective health interventions and policies.

As indicated at the beginning of the text, we focus on the geographic concentration of Mexican Americans in the Southwest as well as their long-time presence in this region, which predates the United States Declaration of Independence. Their large presence in the border region has had a direct impact on the health risk factors they experience. Mexican Americans' historical experience as a colonized people since the annexation of the Southwest by the United States has played an important role in their current social status. Their present-day experiences in schools and the labor market are to a significant degree the result of the history of the American Southwest. This history, in which language issues and racial and ethnic discrimination figure prominently, has had a large impact on the general health of Mexican Americans.

Health does not exist in isolation from historical, socioeconomic, or cultural factors. For example, cultural values, beliefs, and attitudes influence health-seeking behaviors. Cultural values such as **familismo, per-**

sonalismo, confianza, dignidad, and respecto affect the patient-provider relationship, and may influence health care outcomes. It is, therefore, important to understand Mexican Americans' level of **acculturation** in relation to their health. Many of the diseases that we have reviewed are influenced by the Mexican American cultural environment. Cultural issues, therefore, represent an essential part of any prevention and treatment program.

When we look at the health status of Mexican Americans by age we find that children suffer from problems such as underimmunization, **obesity**, and periodontal disease. Adolescents suffer from Type II diabetes and high **mortality** rates due to motor vehicle accidents, homicides, and suicides. Mexican American adolescents also tend to begin sexual activity early, which increases other health risks. Adults also suffer from Type II diabetes, which is correlated with obesity among other factors. Late diagnosis and poor medical management of diabetes in the adult population create additional problems such as vascular disease. This in turn can lead to the amputation of limbs and blindness. Heart disease is the leading cause of death among all racial and ethnic groups in the United States, and cancer is the second leading cause of death among Hispanics. The three most common forms of cancer among Mexican-origin men are lung, colorectal, and prostate cancer. For Mexican-origin women, breast, lung, and colorectal cancer are most common. Lack of knowledge about and access to screenings for these cancers in many cases prevents early diagnosis and effective treatment.

AIDS is the fourth leading cause of death among Hispanics. However, the **epidemiology** of HIV disease is different for Mexican Americans than for other groups. For example, a large number of Mexican-born males contract the virus through male-male sex whereas Mexican-born women acquire the virus primarily through transfusions or sex with an HIV-positive male. Only a small percentage of Mexican-born women acquire HIV through injection drug use. Unfortunately, there are a number of misconceptions concerning HIV transmission among Mexican Americans, and improved outreach and education are needed in this community. Other areas of concern that directly affect the health status of Mexican Americans are prenatal care, domestic violence, occupationally related health issues, and communicable and parasitic diseases related to low-income housing and **occupational location**.

Health care access is a significant issue for all Mexican Americans.

Access refers not only to **financial access** (i.e., health insurance), but also to issues such as the proximity of medical facilities and the availability of culturally and linguistically appropriate care. Although many Americans in the United States are without any form of health insurance, Hispanics comprise an exceptionally large percentage of this uninsured population. In fact, one-third of all Hispanics do not have any form of health insurance, and most of these individuals are of Mexican origin. The major factor influencing health insurance coverage is occupational location. Because many Mexican-origin people are among the **working poor**, a large number are ineligible for publicly subsidized health insurance. At the same time, they do not receive health insurance through their employers, or they cannot afford the insurance that is available. People within the Mexican-origin population who are particularly vulnerable with respect to the lack of health insurance are senior citizens, women, and undocumented **immigrants**. All three groups are vulnerable due to their occupational location, income level, and for the last group, their legal status.

A final important component of health care access concerns the availability of minority health care professionals: doctors, nurses, psychologists, and others. The scarcity of Mexican-origin health care professionals diminishes the quality of health care of Mexican Americans, who are already underserved. Mexican-origin health care professionals play an important role because they are more likely to serve in their respective communities and be able to bridge the gap between the culture of this minority group and that of the health care system. Therefore, increasing the number of Mexican-origin health care professionals will enable greater access to care. **Educational pipeline** programs such as the Hispanic Centers of Excellence are important models that attempt to increase the number of health care professionals.

Other important factors that influence access to quality health care is the degree of **cultural and linguistic competency** of professionals serving people of Mexican descent. Linguistic competency is important to many Mexican immigrants. Monolingual Spanish speakers are at particular risk of not receiving adequate health care. Thus, linguistic competency is an essential component of cultural competency.

Cultural competency requires that individuals who serve the Mexican-origin population understand and be sensitive to the values, practices, and beliefs of this group. Effective communication is a critical component of cultural competency. Cultural competency includes not only the language used by the population, but also sensitivity to the literacy levels of this group and how their cultural and belief system affects their health care practices. There is a considerable amount of literature examining cultural competency but very little of it is specific to those of Mexican origin.

The models that are most frequently used in understanding cultural competency in the health care setting fall into three frameworks: acculturation, therapeutic treatment, and organizational process. All of these models have some limitations with respect to their application to Mexican-origin people. For example, the spectrum of ethnic identity within the Mexican population tends to be reduced to an issue of linguistic skills in Spanish and in English. Given the increasingly complex identity of the Mexican-origin population—which is related to immigrant status, generational status, and regional location—cultural competency models must become more sensitive to the unique characteristics of specific Mexican communities. For example, Mexicans who live in the border regions of Texas or Arizona may have an identity that is closer to that of a Mexican national than say a **Hispano/a** of northern New Mexico. Thus, some cultural and linguistic practices differ substantially.

Cultural competency requires that we look at the mix of our health care providers as well as the support given to individuals who enter the health care system. Although individuals may be trained to be culturally competent, there is still a need for individuals who intuitively understand the culture. Thus, it is important that we continually strive to increase the pool of Mexican-origin health care professionals as well as improve the skills of existing practitioners.

 ## Mexican American Health Policy in the Twenty-First Century

What needs to be done to improve the health status of Mexican Americans? A number of Hispanic health providers and researchers (including the authors of this book) examined this issue in collaboration with the Surgeon General of the United States.[1] The following areas were identified as needing improvement:

1. Improved access to health care
2. Improved data collection strategies
3. Increased representation in the sciences and health professions

4. Development of a relevant and comprehensive research agenda
5. Culturally appropriate health promotion and disease prevention programs

Problems identified in the area of health care access were:

1. Lack of comprehensive and portable health care coverage
2. Underrepresentation of Hispanics in leadership positions affecting public policy
3. Lack of adequate and available health care service delivery systems and infrastructure to address **primary, secondary,** and **tertiary** health care needs of Hispanics
4. Lack of accessible and adequate health care facilities due to financial, cultural, and linguistic barriers

Problems identified in the area of data collection included:

1. Inadequate inclusion of Hispanics in data systems
2. Lack of data specific to Hispanic health issues
3. Limited awareness of and access to local, state, and federal databases
4. Lack of quality, accurate, timely, and culturally sensitive data system design, collection efforts, analysis, and replication
5. Poor coordination of efforts in health data collection by local, state, and federal agencies

Problems identified with respect to representation in the health professions were:

1. The underrepresentation of Hispanics at all levels of the health professions
2. The underrepresentation of Hispanics in the educational pipeline of the health professions, as well as inadequate levels of funding for Hispanics in health and science education programs
3. The underutilization of linguistically and culturally competent foreign-educated Hispanic health professionals

Problems identified in the research agenda issue were:

1. Underfunding of Hispanic health research initiatives
2. Lack of culturally appropriate theories, models, and methodologies
3. Underrepresentation of Hispanics at all levels of research activities

4. Lack of coordination among diverse areas of investigation

Problems identified in the health promotion and disease prevention area include:

1. A weak infrastructure for training in health promotion and disease prevention
2. Lack of proven models for comprehensive, culturally competent, and community-specific primary, secondary, and tertiary prevention programs
3. Lack of public-private partnerships in support of health promotion and disease prevention goals
4. Lack of diffusion of culturally appropriate health promotion and disease prevention models
5. A general lack of awareness on the part of media and the public about Hispanic health promotion and disease prevention issues
6. Lack of cooperation in addressing environmental hazards that affect health promotion and disease prevention

All of these areas can be addressed—and eventually resolved—through a concerted effort involving local, state, and national health policymakers in collaboration with Hispanic health professionals and the community at large. The future of the United States depends on a healthy, educated, and motivated citizenry. This text has highlighted important issues that need to be addressed in order for people of Mexican origin to overcome the obstacles they have faced in the past so that they can continue to make important contributions in the twenty-first century.

■ **Note**

1. Novello, A. *Recommendations to the Surgeon General to Improve Hispanic/Latino Health.* Washington, D.C.: U.S. Department of Health and Human Services, Office of the Surgeon General, June 1993.

■ GLOSSARY

acculturation: The degree to which Mexican Americans adopt mainstream, Euro-American values and customs. It usually refers to the dual learning of two cultures—Mexican American and Euro-American.

acculturative stress: Psychosocial stress associated with the process of modifying one's culture through contact with another culture group (acculturation) or in adapting to the dominant culture.

AIDS (acquired immunodeficiency syndrome): Disease of the human immune system that is caused by infection with HIV.

allopathic: Describes an approach to medicine that views the physician as an active interventionist. A physician who practices this type of medicine attempts to counteract the effect of a disease by using surgical or medical treatments that produce effects opposite to those of the disease.

American Association of Medical Colleges: An organization of allopathic colleges of medicine in the United States and Canada.

attributable risk: The rate of disease that can be directly linked to exposure to a disease.[1]

backloading: A means of sharing drugs by squirting part of the drug solution into the back of the syringe.

behavioral epidemiology: A specialty in the field of epidemiology; it focuses on risk behaviors that contribute to spreading disease.

bicultural: Having the ability to operate in two cultures. This requires skill in the language, knowledge of cultural norms and the ability to switch between the expectations of two distinct cultures.

bilingual: Having or using two languages. The fluency of a native speaker is implied in the definition.[2]

bilis: A hot, dry condition; it is "caused by the excess secretion of bile that floods the system when a person is suffering from chronic rage."[3]

birth rate: The number of live births per 1,000 women in a population.[4]

Chicanas/os: People of Mexican American descent who have re-evaluated how their ethnic awareness affects the way they see themselves within the Mexican American and broader communities.

code switch: The ability to shift between two languages or dialects based on the ethnic makeup of a specific group in order to appropriately match the expected communication style of that group.

confianza: A sense of confidence or trust in one's health care provider or physician; the establishment of a trusting, safe, and open bond between two people.

co-occurrence: Things that happen together or simultaneously.

cooker: A spoon, bottle cap, or concave part of an aluminum can that is used to heat, dissolve, and rinse a drug solution.

cotton: Fabric used to filter a solution of drugs before injection.[5]

cultural competency: The acceptance and respect for cultural differences. To be culturally competent, medical staff must self-assess their attitudes and agency policies regarding culture, must pay careful attention to the dynamics of difference, must continually expand their cultural knowledge and resources, and must change their service models in order to better meet the needs of minority populations.

curandera/o: A folk healer whose practice of healing is based on the use of native plants and herbs in curative potions and the laying on of the hands. This method of healing is widespread in South America, the Caribbean, and the southwestern United States.

de facto segregation: Segregation that is actual but is not necessarily supported by or enforceable by law or legislation.

de jure segregation: Segregation that is supported by or enforceable by law, legislation, or administrative policies.

dignidad: A Mexican American's personal sense of dignity; it should not be violated by a physician or by health care in general.

educational attainment: The highest grade completed or the highest educational degree obtained by an individual. The average education level of a population group can be calculated using these data.[6]

educational pipeline: An academic path to a career in health sciences. To increase the number of minorities in a field, the educational pipeline ideally would have grade schools with large minority enrollments, colleges interested in increasing the number of minority graduates going on to medical school or postgraduate study in health sciences, and "academic medical centers" (medical schools and other health professional schools) that want to improve opportunities for minority students and health care professionals.[7]

efficacy in treatment: The ability or power to give cost-effective treatment that results in the best possible health outcomes.

empacho: A swollen belly resulting from undigested food.

epidemic: The widespread outbreak of a disease affecting either large numbers of persons in a specific population or a relatively small area.

epidemiological: Of or relating to *epidemiology,* which is the study of disease patterns and distributions in human groups.

epidemiological patterns: Risk factors, risk behaviors, incidence rates and prevalence rates of disease.

epidemiological profile: A complete picture of how a population group is affected by disease. It is based on a combination of risk factors, risk behaviors, and incidence and prevalence rates.

epidemiology: The study of disease patterns and distributions in human populations.

ethnic enclaves: Migrants or immigrants of similar background or from the same region that reside close together. Generally, enclaves are sites of mutual assistance, where residents share resources and information with each other.[8]

etiology: All of the causes of a disease or condition.

familismo: The cultural belief that places family needs above individual needs and desires.

federal poverty level (FPL): The guideline for determining poverty in the United States. In the forty-eight states and Washington, D.C., a family of four is considered to live in poverty if their annual income is at or below the federal poverty line of $16,700.[9]

feminization of poverty: A term that describes the increasing numbers of single-parent households where women are the head of the household. An overly large number of these women and their children are living in poverty.

fertility rate: The number of live births per 1,000 women age fifteen to forty-four in a specified population group.[10]

financial access: The ability either to pay for private health insurance or to qualify for free or low-cost public health care coverage.

foreign-born: All U.S. residents who were not born either in the United States or a U.S. territory or to a parent who is a U.S. citizen.[11]

frío de la matriz: This term literally translates as "cold womb or cold uterus." It is a folk disease that is recognized after a mother has given birth (postpartum). It is believed to be caused by insufficient rest after delivery. Symptoms include pelvic congestion, menstrual irregularities, and loss of libido.

frontloading: The process of drawing a drug solution from a cotton or cooker through the needle of a syringe.

Gadsden Purchase: A piece of land that the United States bought from Mexico for $10 million in 1853. It is named after Senator James Gadsden, who negotiated the sale. Measuring about 30,000 square miles, it includes what is today southern New Mexico and southern Arizona.[12]

health care access: The opportunity to obtain and pay for health care services and procedures; minorities generally have less access to health care than non-minorities. Access is often affected by income, employment, and language status.[13]

health insurance premium: The price of insurance protection for a specified risk for a specified period of time. Many health insurance plans require payment of monthly premiums.[14]

health status: A measure of an individual's or a population's health based on many psychological and physical factors, such as mortality and morbidity rates (number of deaths and number of people with diseases which may cause death). Health status varies greatly among different ethnic groups and is related to income, educational attainment, and race/ethnicity.[15]

healthy migrant hypothesis: The idea that migrants from Mexico are generally healthier than other American minority populations. This is an attempt to explain the Mexican American mortality-morbidity paradox (that is, the fact that Mexican Americans have lower rates of death and serious illness than other minority groups).

Hippocratic-Galenic beliefs: Beliefs that come from Greek humoral theory (proposed by Hippocrates) and expanded upon by Galen (a Roman physician). This theory says that there are four humors, or fluids, in the body: black bile, yellow bile, blood, and phlegm. An imbalance in these four humors was believed to cause certain illnesses.

Hispanic: Of, relating to, or being a person of Latin American descent living in the United States. It includes people of Cuban, Mexican, Puerto Rican, Central American, or South American origin.

Hispano/a: A native or resident of the U.S. Southwest who is a descendant of Spaniards who settled in the area before it was taken over by the United States. It is most often used to refer to long-time Hispanic residents of New Mexico.[16]

HIV (human immunodeficiency virus): One of a group of viruses called retroviruses. HIV gradually destroys certain white blood cells called T-helper lymphocytes. The result is that the body cannot control viruses or bacteria that the normal immune system keeps in check easily. AIDS (acquired immunodeficiency syndrome) refers to the disease process caused by HIV infection.[17]

home health agency: A business that arranges for health care professionals to examine and treat patients in their own homes.

Hopwood decision: The 1996 ruling that the affirmative action admissions policy of the University of Texas law school had resulted in discrimination against four white applicants. This decision resulted in the removal of all affirmative action programs in Texas institutions of higher education as illegal. "Race neutral" policies were put in place to determine admission, financial aid, scholarships, recruitment, and retention programs.[18]

immigrants: A category of foreign-born people who come to the United States from another country to live for an indefinite period of time; not all foreign-born persons are immigrants. Presumably, immigrants desire, even if they do not actively seek, legal status leading to permanent residency or citizenship.[19]

incidence: The number of new cases of an illness or disease that occurs in a certain population at a particular time. It measures how many people are currently becoming infected or affected by a disease and is one measure of morbidity.[20]

inpatient care: Health care procedures that require the patient to stay in the hospital for a time. It is the opposite of outpatient treatment.

la sufrida: The "suffering" woman; la sufrida is based on the concept of marianismo, a Hispanic cultural expectation that women should be self-sacrificing.

Latina/o: A person who is a native or inhabitant of Western Hemisphere countries that are south of the United States, including Mexico, Central and South America, and the Caribbean; it also applies to a person living in the United States who comes, or whose ancestors come, from one of these countries.

linguistic competency: The ability to speak, read, and write the language of a specific population and also to understand the nuances of the region, class position, and preferred dialect of the specific group.

longitudinal data: Data that are collected over a long period of time. The same measures are collected on the same individuals at set intervals over a span of years. Longitudinal data allow one to understand how a problem develops and progresses.

machismo: Manliness and virility. The lighter side of machismo within Hispanic cultures is personified by the *caballero* (gentleman) who is responsible for the welfare of his family and protects the honor of his wife and family. It is also associated with a man's sexual prowess with women. Machismo is expressed in romanticism and a jealous guarding of one's wife or fiance, as well as premarital and extramarital affairs.

mal de ojo: An illness caused by being stared at; usually perceived in children or babies who have been paid more attention than usual; the illness also has a supernatural component.[21]

malinchismo: A concept that embodies the historical role of Malinche or Doña Marina, the Aztec princess who served as Cortés' interpreter, guide, and mistress during the conquest of Mexico. It is sometimes used as a negative term describing Mexican-origin women who are seen as traitors against Mexican culture or the Mexican-origin community.

marianismo: The female counterpart of *machismo*. Taken from the name Mary, it is based on the figure of the Virgin Mother within the Catholic religion. Women are expected to suffer in silence with regard to the sexual double standard and their husband's affairs, to place their children and husband' needs above their own, and to be the overseer of the home and family (including health care issues).

matriculants: Applicants to a medical or other school who have been accepted to the school and have chosen to enroll there.

Medicaid: A jointly funded, federal-state health insurance program for low-income and needy people. It covers about thirty-six million people, including children; people who are elderly, blind, or disabled; and people who are eligible for federal income maintenance payments (welfare, ssi).[22]

medically indigent: Describes a person who is too poor to pay for medical care. Some states choose not to participate in Medicare and instead operate their own medically indigent health programs, which do not receive federal funding. State medically indigent programs may provide both cash and medical assistance, or medical assistance only.[23]

Medicare: The nation's largest health insurance program, covering thirty-nine million Americans. It provides health insurance to people age sixty-five and over, those with permanent kidney failure, and certain people with disabilities. To be eligible for Medicare, an individual or his/her spouse must have worked for at least ten years in Medicare-covered employment, be at least sixty-five years of age, and be a citizen or permanent resident of the United States.[24]

metropolitan area: A geographic area of large population. It includes a core city (or cities) and nearby communities that are socially and economically connected to it. For example, a metropolitan area could be comprised of an urbanized city and the communities from which the city's workers commute.[25]

Mexican Americans: Persons of Mexican descent born and residing in the United States.

modifiable risk factors: Health behaviors that put a person at risk for illness but that can be adjusted or changed to lower the risk. Examples are lifestyle choices such as smoking, lack of exercise, and poor diet.

morbidity: The number of people in a population at any given time who have a particular disease, illness, or injury; the rate of incidence of a disease.[26]

mortality: The number of deaths in a population for a given period of time.[27]

native-born: A U.S. resident born within the United States or in a U.S. territory (for example, Puerto Rico), or born in a foreign country to an American citizen.[28]

natural history of disease: "The stages that a disease goes through in the course of growth, infection and illness, death, or recovery."[29]

non-Hispanic: People who do not identify themselves as Mexican American, Chicano/a, Mexican, Mexicano/a, Puerto Rican, Cuban, Central American, South American, or other Hispanic.[30]

non-insulin-dependent diabetes mellitus (NIDDM): The most common form of diabetes mellitus; about 90 to 95 percent of people who have diabetes have NIDDM, also called Type II diabetes. Unlike the insulin-dependent type of diabetes (Type I), in which the pancreas makes no insulin, people with non-insulin-dependent diabetes produce some insulin, sometimes even large amounts. However, either their bodies do not produce enough insulin or their body cells do not take in insulin properly. People with NIDDM can often control their condition through diet, exercise, and weight loss.[31]

obesity: The state of being significantly overweight. Anyone who is more than 20 percent over his or her ideal weight is considered obese.[32]

occupational location: The type of job and sector of employment (e.g., manufacturing, service) in which a person is employed.

outpatient health services: Health care procedures that can be done without an overnight stay in a hospital.

Pap smear: A test for cancer in the female genital tract in which a small sample of cells is scraped off the cervix for testing. It is recommended for all women over eighteen and for younger women who are sexually active.

partera: Midwife.

patchwork providers: A loose association of health care providers that provide health care services for the underinsured or uninsured in a given region.

personalismo: "The ability to forge and maintain affiliations and relationships as a means of connecting meaningfully to other people."[33]

predictor variables: The influencing factors used to forecast or identify a particular relationship between the past and future occurrence of a behavior or to determine a pattern of behavior.

prevalence: The number of people in a certain population at a certain time who have a given disease or injury; the "measurement of morbidity at a point in time." Whereas incidence measures only new cases of a disease or illness, prevalence measures all the people affected by that condition, no matter how long they have had it.[34]

primary prevention: Efforts to stop a disease before it occurs; "health promotion, health education, and health protection are three main facets of primary prevention."[35]

process evaluation: Assessments obtained during health promotion activities that are used to control, provide feedback, or improve the quality of performance or delivery of the program.

Proposition 187:   A 1994 ballot initiative passed in California; it proposed to prohibit undocumented immigrants from being eligible for or receiving public social services, public education, and non-emergency health care services (including prenatal and elder care). It also required state and local agencies to report persons thought to be undocumented to the California attorney general and the United States Immigration and Naturalization Service. This measure has since been struck down in court as unconstitutional.[36]

Proposition 209:   A 1996 initiative to do away with affirmative action programs and policies in all state and local governments, districts, public universities, colleges, schools, and other government agencies in the state of California.[37]

psychologically inoculate: To provide resistance skills that lower the risk for using drugs.

racialized: A situation in which groups are defined or categorized based on biological identifying characteristics.

razalogía: The empowerment of *raza* communities (Hispanic or Latino/a). "It challenges each individual community member to identify, contrast and compare, and then reject concepts and behaviors which weaken their resolution to act on behalf of the community's well-being."[38]

relative risk: The risk of disease or death in a population exposed to a health condition divided by the risk of disease or death in the unexposed population.

rented needles: Needles that are rented for a small fee, usually from a "shooting gallery," which is a place where users can rent paraphernalia to inject drugs, though the drugs themselves usually cannot be bought there.

respeto: Mutual respect between physician and patient that should be maintained; implies professionalism and understanding of boundaries in the relationship; the need to maintain one's personal integrity and that of others.

rinse water: Water that is used to flush out or rinse a syringe before or after use.

salmon bias hypothesis: The idea that Mexican-origin persons return to Mexico to die, preventing them from being recorded in death statistics;

this is an attempt to explain the Mexican American mortality-morbidity paradox (that is, the fact that Mexican Americans have lower rates of death and serious illness than other minority groups).

secondary prevention: Efforts to screen for or detect a disease or illness in an early stage to prevent it from progressing to an impairment or disability.[39]

seroprevalence: A measure of the prevalence or extent of the HIV virus in the blood of a particular population.

simpatía: A state in which social interactions are smooth and positive.

sobadora: A healer who practices massage therapy using spiritual or religious principles.

speedball: An injected mixture of heroin and cocaine.[40]

subjective culture: The non-physical aspects of a culture, including attitudes, norms, values, beliefs, and expectancies.

subpopulation: An identifiable section or subdivision of a population.[41]

Supplemental Security Income (SSI):   A federal program that provides income to people who are sixty-five or older, blind, or disabled and who have few assets or little income. Children are included.[42]

susto: "Fright of the soul"; "soul loss" due to a frightening or traumatic event.[43]

syncretism: The mixture or combination of different cultural or religious forms of belief, practice, or ritual.

tertiary prevention: Efforts designed to slow or stop the progression of a disability, condition, or disorder in order to minimize the amount of care required.[44]

Treaty of Guadalupe Hidalgo: The peace treaty that ended the Mexican War on February 2, 1848, signed in the town of Guadalupe Hidalgo outside Mexico City. It granted Texas to the United States and officially set the U.S.-Mexico border at the Rio Grande. Mexico also ceded California and the land that would become the states of Nevada and Utah, as well as parts of present-day Arizona, New Mexico, Colorado, and Wyoming. The United States paid Mexico $15 million for this territory. The treaty also promised that Mexicans living in the territory ceded to the United States would receive full rights as U.S. citizens.[45]

variable: In scientific research, a measurable element or factor that does or might influence an outcome or situation. For example, variables influencing health status include occupational location, socioeconomic status, immigrant status, and educational attainment.

voluntary system of health insurance: A system that deducts an amount from an individual's paycheck and allows the person to pay into a private health insurance plan instead of being forced to participate in the program provided by the employer.

working poor: Individuals who are active in the labor force but do not receive fringe benefits such as health insurance and do not qualify for public subsidy programs such as Medicare. These individuals are most likely to fall in the category of the underinsured and uninsured within the health care system.

■ Notes

1. T. C. Timmreck, *Health Services Cyclopedic Dictionary,* 3d ed. (Boston: Jones and Bartlett Publishers, 1997).

2. *Webster's Third New International Dictionary of the English Language, Unabridged* (Springfield, Mass.: Merriam-Webster, 1986).

3. E. Ávila, *Woman Who Glows in the Dark: A Curandera Reveals Traditional Aztec Secrets of Physical and Spiritual Health.* (New York: Jeremy P. Tarcher/Putnam, 1999), pp. 24, 44.

4. National Center for Health Statistics, *Health, United States, 1993.* Available from the NCHS web site: http://www.cdc.gov/nchswww/data/hus_93.pdf.

5. University of Indiana drug prevention resource web site: http://www.drugs.indiana.edu/cgi-bin/scripts/engine.pl.

6. U.S. Census Bureau web site: http://www.census.gov/population/www/cps/cpsdef.html.

7. Association of American Medical Colleges web site: http://www.aamc.org/meded/minority/3x2/fouryear.htm.

8. Juan Vicente Palerm and Matt T. Salo, "Immigrant and Migrant Farm Workers in the Santa Maria Valley, California," U.S. Census Bureau Research Report #EX95/21, 1995. Available from http://www.census.gov/srd/www/byyear.html.

9. Department of Health and Human Services web site: http://aspe.os.dhhs.gov/poverty/99poverty.htm.

10. National Center for Health Statistics, *Health, United States, 1993.* Available from NCHS web site: http://www.cdc.gov/nchswww/data/hus_93.pdf.

11. U.S. Census Bureau web site: www.census.gov/population/www/documentation/twps0029/twps0029.html#sources.

12. *The Columbia Encyclopedia,* 5th ed., (New York: Columbia University Press, n.d.). Accessed at cbs News web site: http://cbs.infoplease.com/ce5/CE019890.html.

13. U.S. Department of Health and Human Services, Public Health Service and Health Resources and Services Administration. *Health Status of Minorities and Low-Income Groups.* 3d ed. (Washington, D.C.: Government Printing Office, 1991), pp. 6, 8, 331.

14. Yahoo Insurance Glossary web site: http://gen.insweb.yahoo.com/general/ref/general-p.htm.

15. J. Rapoport, R. L. Robertson, and B. Stuart, *Understanding Health Economics.* (Rockville, Md.: Aspen Publications, 1982), p. 100. U.S. Department of Health and Human Services, *Health Status of Minorities,* pp. 6, 8, 331.

16. *Webster's Third New International Dictionary.*

17. Texas A&M University web site: http://resi.tamu.edu/history1.htm.

18. U.S. Department of Justice, Drug Enforcement Administration web site: www.usdoj.gov/dea/pubs/abuse/chap8/aids.htm.

19. U.S. Census Bureau web site: http://www.census.gov/population/www/documentation/twps0022/twps0022.html.

20. Timmreck, *Health Services Cyclopedic Dictionary,* p. 330.

21. Ávila, *Woman Who Glows in the Dark,* pp. 58–60.

22. Health Care Financing Administration web site: http://www.hcfa.gov/medicaid/medicaid.htm.

23. Milliman and Robertson Actuaries and Consultants web site: http://www.blueworld.com/milliman/publications/reports/understanding_medicaid/overview.html.

24. Medicare web site: http://www.medicare.gov/whatis.html.

25. U.S. Census Bureau web site: http://www.census.gov/population/www/documentation/twps0006/twps0006.html.

26. Timmreck, *Health Services Cyclopedic Dictionary,* p. 451.

27. Ibid.

28. U.S. Census Bureau web site: www.census.gov/population/www/documentation/twps0029/twps0029.html#sources.

29. Timmreck, *Health Services Cyclopedic Dictionary,* p. 464.

30. U.S. Census Bureau web site: http://www.census.gov/population/www/socdemo/hispanic/hispdef97.html.

31. National Institutes of Health web site: www.niddk.nih.gov/health/diabetes/pubs/dmdict/dmdict.htm.

32. MedicineNet online medical dictionary: www.medicinenet.com.

33. R. M. Gil and C. I. Vázquez, *The Maria Paradox: How Latinas Can Merge Old World Traditions with New World Self-Esteem* (New York: Perigee Books, 1996), p. 16.

34. Timmreck, *Health Services Cyclopedic Dictionary,* p. 573.

35. Timmreck, *Health Services Cyclopedic Dictionary,* p. 574.

36. California Secretary of State's Office web site: http://ca94.election.digital.com/e/prop/187/home.html.

37. California Attorney General's Office web site: http://Vote96.ss.ca.gov/Vote96/html/BP/209.htm.

38. S. J. Andrade and C. Doria-Ortiz, "Nuestro Bienestar: A Mexican-American Community-Based Definition of Health Promotion in the Southwestern United States," *Drugs: Education, Prevention, and Policy* 2, no. 2 (1995): p. 135.

39. Timmreck, *Health Services Cyclopedic Dictionary,* p. 575.

40. University of Indiana drug prevention web site: http://www.drugs.indiana.edu/cgi-bin/scripts/engine.pl.

41. *Webster's Third New International Dictionary.*

42. Social Security Administration web site: http://www.ssa.gov/pubs/faq.html.

43. Ávila, *Woman Who Glows in the Dark,* pp. 64, 185.

44. Timmreck, *Health Services Cyclopedic Dictionary,* p. 575.

45. *The Columbia Encyclopedia,* accessed at CBS News web site: http://cbs.infoplease.com/ce5/CE022115.html.

■ BIBLIOGRAPHY

Abraido-Lanza, A. F., B. P. Dohrenwend, D. S. Ng-Mak, and J. B. Turner. "The Latino Mortality Paradox: A Test of the 'Salmon Bias' and Healthy Migrant Hypotheses." *American Journal of Public Health* 89 (1999).

Ahmad, N. "Civil Rights Groups Sue UC Berkeley." The Daily Californian, U-Wire, City College of San Francisco web site: www.ccsf.cc.ca.us/Events_Pubs/Guards man/s990208/uwire02.shtml.

Alfaro, P. "Horizontes Laredo Indigenous Outreach Project." In *Community-Based* AIDS Prevention, pp. 15–17. DHHS Pub. No. (ADM) 91-7752. Washington, D.C.: U.S. Department of Health and Human Services, 1991.

Alvarez, R. *Latino Community Mental Health.* Spanish Speaking Mental Health Research and Development Program Monograph No. Los Angeles: University of California at Los Angeles, 1974.

American Nurses Association web site: www.ana.org/readroom/fsdemogr.htm#Eth nic/RacialBackground.

Andrade, S. J., and C. Doria-Ortiz. "Nuestro Bienestar: A Mexican-American Community-Based Definition of Health Promotion in the Southwestern United States." *Drugs: Education, Prevention, and Policy* 2, no. 2 (1995).

Arizona Health Care Cost Containment System web site: http://170.68.21.47/Con tent/Resources/AnnRpt97/appendix/apndxB.htm.

Association of American Medical Colleges. *Facts: Applicants, Matriculants, and Graduates, 1991–1997.* U.S. 1997/1998 ed. Washington, D.C.: AAMC, 1998.

——. *Project 3000 by 2000 Progress to Date: Year Four Progress Report.* Washington D.C.: Association of American Medical Colleges, Division of Community and Minority Programs, 1996.

Ávila, E., and J. Parker. *Woman Who Glows in the Dark.* New York: Jeremy P. Tarcher/Putnam, 1999.

Barrera, M. *Race and Class in the Southwest: A Theory of Racial Inequality.* Notre Dame, Ind.: University of Notre Dame Press, 1979.

Barzansky, B., H. S. Jonas, and S. I. Etzel. "Education Programs in U.S. Medical Schools, 1997–1998." *Journal of the American Medical Association* 280 (1998), pp. 803–8.

Bayer, R. "AIDS Prevention and Cultural Sensitivity: Are They Compatible?" *American Journal of Public Health* 84 (1994), pp. 895–98.

Bolen, J. C., L. Rhodes, E. E. Powell-Griner, S. D. Bland, and D. Holtzman. "State-Specific Prevalence of Selected Health Behaviors, by Race and Ethnicity—Behavioral Risk Factor Surveillance System, 1997." *Mortality and Morbidity Weekly Report* 49(SS02) (March 24, 2000), pp. 1–60.

Booth, R. E. et al. "HIV Risk-Related Sex Behaviors among Injection Drug Users,

Crack Smokers, and Injection Drug Users Who Smoke Crack." *American Journal of Public Health* 83, no. 8 (1993), pp. 1144–48.

Botvin, G. J. et al. "The Effectiveness of Culturally Focused and Generic Skills Training Approaches to Alcohol and Drug Abuse Prevention among Minority Youth." *Psychology of Addictive Behaviors* 8 (1994), pp. 116–27.

Boyko, E. J. et al. "Higher Insulin and C-peptide Concentrations in Hispanic Populations at High Risk for NIDDM: San Luis Valley Diabetes Study." *Diabetes* 40 (1991).

C' de Baca, J. "Inheritance Awaits San Luis Residents and Relatives," *La Voz de Colorado* 11, no. 21 (May 24, 1995).

Casas, J. M. "A Culturally Sensitive Model for Evaluating Alcohol and Other Drug Abuse Prevention Programs: A Hispanic Perspective." In *Cultural Competence for Evaluators: A Guide for Alcohol and Other Drug Abuse Prevention Practitioners Working With Ethnic/Racial Communities,* eds. M. A. Orlandi, R. Weston, and L. G. Epstein, pp. 75–116. Rockville, Md.: U.S. Department of Health and Human Services, Public Health Service, Alcohol, Drug Abuse, and Mental Health Administration, 1992.

Center for Substance Abuse Prevention. *Advanced Methodological Issues in Culturally Competent Evaluation for Substance Abuse Prevention.* Health Resources and Services Administration Bureau of Primary Health Care. Rockville, Md.: U.S. Department of Health and Human Services, 1996.

Centers for Disease Control and Prevention (CDC). *The Health of America's Youth: Current Trends in Health Status and Health Services.* Atlanta, Ga: CDC, 1991.

——. *HIV/AIDS Surveillance Report.* Year-end ed. vol. 10, no. 2. Washington, D.C.: U.S. Department of Health and Human Services, Public Health Service, December 1998.

——. "Self-Reported Prevalence of Diabetes among Hispanics—United States, 1994–1997." *Mortality and Morbidity Weekly Report* 48, no. 1 (1999).

Chávez, E. L., R. Edwards, and E. R. Oetting. "Mexican American and White American Dropouts' Drug Use, Health Status, and Involvement in Violence." *Public Health Reports* 104, no. 6 (1986), pp. 594–604.

Chávez, E. L., and R. C. Swain. "An Epidemiological Comparison of Mexican American and White Non-Hispanic 8th and 12th Grade Students' Substance Use." *American Journal of Public Health* 82 (1992), pp. 445–47.

Chávez, E. L. et al. "Drug Use by Small-Town Mexican American Youth: A Pilot Study." *Hispanic Journal of Behavioral Science* 8, no. 3 (1986), pp. 243–58.

Cohen, J. B. et al. "Women and IV Drugs: Parental and Heterosexual Transmission of Human Immunodeficiency Virus. *Journal of Drug Issues* 19, no. 1 (1989), pp. 39–56.

Cohen, L. M. "*Controlarse* and the Problems of Life among Latino Immigrants." In *Stress and Hispanic Mental Health: Relating Research to Service Delivery,* pp. 202–18. DHHS Pub. No. (ADM) 85-141. Washington, D.C.: U.S. Department of Health and Human Services, 1985.

Colorado Department of Health Care Policy and Financing web site: www.chcpf
.state.co.us/refmat/99RefMan-3.html#EES-6.

COSSMHO (National Coalition of Hispanic Health and Human Service Organizations)
HIV/AIDS—The Impact on Hispanics in Selected States. Washington, D.C.: COSSMHO,
1991.

Cuellar, I., B. Arnold, and R. Moldonado. "Acculturation Rating Scale for Mexican
Americans–II: A Revision of the Original ARSMA Scale." *Hispanic Journal of Behavioral Sciences* 17, no. 3 (1995).

Dávila, A., A. K. Bohara, and R. Saenz. "Accent Penalties and the Earnings of
Mexican Americans." *Social Science Quarterly* 74, no. 4 (December 1993).

Davis, S. M., and M. B. Harris. "Sexual Knowledge, Sexual Interests, and Sources of
Sexual Information of Rural and Urban Adolescents from Three Cultures." *Adolescence* 17, no. 66 (1982), pp. 471–92.

Dawson, D. A., and A. M. Hardy. "AIDS Knowledge and Attitudes among Hispanic
Americans: Provisional Data from the 1988 National Health Interview Survey."
NCHS Advance Data 166 (1990), pp. 1–22.

De Anda, D., R. M. Becerra, and P. Fielder. "Sexuality, Pregnancy, and Motherhood
among Mexican American Adolescents." *Journal of Adolescent Research* 3 (1988).

de la Torre, A. "Hard Choices and Changing Roles among Mexican Migrant Campe-
sinas." In *Building with Our Hands: New Directions in Chicana Studies,* eds. A. de la
Torre and B. M. Pesquera, pp. 168–78. Berkeley and Los Angeles: University of
California Press, 1993.

de la Torre, A., R. Friis, H. R. Hunter, and L. García. "The Health Insurance Status
of U.S. Latino Women: A Profile from the 1982–1984 HHANES." *American Journal of
Public Health* 86, no. 4 (April 1996).

De la Trinidad, M. "Mexican Americans in Education: Segregation in the Southwest
Schools, 1930–1976." Unpublished seminar paper, Department of History, University of Arizona, 1998.

Dembo, R. et al. "Psychosocial, Substance Abuse, and Delinquency Differences
among Anglo, Hispanic, and African American Male Youths Entering a Juvenile
Assessment Center." *Substance Use and Misuse* 33, no. 7 (1998), pp. 1481–1510.

Department of Health and Human Services web site: http://aspe.os.dhhs.gov/poverty/
99poverty.htm.

Des Jarlais, D. C. et al. "Heterosexual Partners: A Large Risk Group for AIDS [letter].
Lance 2, no. 8415 (1984), pp. 1346–47.

Díaz, T., J. W. Buehler, K. G. Castro, and J. W. Ward. "AIDS Trends among Hispanics
in the United States." *American Journal of Public Health* 83 (1993).

DiClemente, R. J., C. B. Boyer, and E. S. Morales. "Minorities and AIDS: Knowledge,
Attitudes and Misconceptions among Black and Hispanic Adolescents." *American
Journal of Public Health* 78, no. 1 (1988), pp. 55–57.

"Eliminating Racial and Ethnic Disparities in Health." Washington, D.C.: Grant Makers in Health, September 1998.

Espinosa, K. E., and D. S. Massey. "Determinants of English Proficiency among Mexican Migrants to the United States." *International Migration Review* 31, no. 1 (spring 1997).

Espinosa, P. "The Border" (series broadcast on PBS). Available from Public Broadcasting Service web site: www.pbs.org/kpbs/theborder.

Estrada, A. L. "Behavioral Epidemiology of HIV Risks among Injection Drug Users: Comparative Assessment." Paper presented at the HIV-AIDS Health Services Research and Delivery Conference, Agency for Health Care Policy and Research, Miami, Fla., December 1991.

——. "Deriving Culturally Competent HIV Prevention Models for Mexican American Injection Drug Users." In *National Institute on Drug Abuse Conference,* AIDS Prevention Intervention among Minority Injecting Drug Users: Collected Papers. Washington, D.C.: U.S. Department of Health and Human Services, April 1992.

——. "Drug Use and HIV Risks among African-American, Mexican-American, and Puerto Rican Drug Injectors." *Journal of Psychoactive Drugs* 30, no. 3 (1998), 247–53.

——. "HIV Risk Behaviors among Gay Latinos Residing in the U.S.-Mexico Border Area." Paper presented at the 120th Annual Meeting of the American Public Health Association, Washington, D.C., April 1992.

Estrada, A. L., J. R. Erickson, S. J. Stevens, and P. J. Glider. "AIDS Risk Behaviors among Straight and Gay IVDUs: A Comparative Analysis." Paper presented at the Second Annual National AIDS Demonstration and Research NADR Conference, Bethesda, Md., November 1990.

Estrada, A. L. et al. "HIV Risk Behaviors among Mexican-Origin and Anglo Female Intravenous Drug Users." *Border Health* 7, no. 1 (1991), pp. 1–4.

"Excerpts from Don and Mike's Messages of Hatred to Hispanics," *Hispanic Link Weekly Report* 17, no. 34 (August 30, 1999).

Flack, J. M., H. Amaro, W. Jenkins, et al. "Epidemiology of Minority Health." *Health Psychology* 14, no. 7 (1995).

Flora, J. A., and C. E. Thoresen. "Reducing the Risk of AIDS in Adolescents." *American Psychologist* 43, no. 11 (1988), pp. 965–70.

Freire, P. *Pedagogy of the Oppressed.* New York: Continuum, 1995.

Friedman-Jiménez, G., and J. S. Ortiz. "Occupational Health" Chap. 12 in *Latino Health in the United States: A Growing Challenge,* eds. C. W. Molina and M. Aguirre-Molina. Washington, D.C.: American Public Health Association, 1994.

Gavira, M., and G. Stem. "Problems in Designing and Implementing Culturally Relevant Mental Health Services for Latinos in the United States." *Social Science Medicine* 14B (1980), pp. 65–71.

Gergen, P. J., T. Ezzati, and H. Russell. "DTP Immunization Status and Tetanus

Antitoxin Status of Mexican American Children Ages Six Months through Eleven Years." *American Journal of Public Health* 78 (1988).

Giachello, A. "Maternal/Perinatal Health." Chap. 6 in *Latino Health in the United States: A Growing Challenge,* eds. C. W. Molina and M. Aguirre-Molina. Washington, D.C.: American Health Association, 1994.

Ginzburg, H. M. "Intravenous Drug Users and the Acquired Immune Deficiency Syndrome." *Public Health Reports* 99 (1984), pp. 206–12.

Glaser, H. S., and K. L. Jones. "Non-insulin Dependent Diabetes Mellitus in Mexican American Children." *Western Journal of Medicine* 168, no. 1 (1998).

Gutiérrez, D. G. *Walls and Mirrors.* Berkeley: University of California Press, 1995.

Guyer, J., and C. Mann. "Employed but Not Insured: A State-by-State Analysis of the Number of Low-Income Working Parents Who Lack Health Insurance." Washington, D.C.: Center on Budget and Policy Priorities, 1999. Available from the Center on Budget and Policy Priorities web site: http://www.cbpp.org/2-9-99mcaid.htm.

Haffner, S. M., M. P. Stern, F. D. Hazuda, et al. "Role of Obesity and Fat Distribution in Non-insulin Dependent Diabetes Mellitus in Mexican Americans and Non-Hispanic Whites." *Diabetes Care* 9 (1986).

Hamamoto, D. Y., and R. Torres. *New American Destinies: A Reader in Contemporary Asian and Latino Immigration.* New York: Routledge, 1997.

Harris, M., D. E. Goldstein, K. M. Flegal, et al. "Prevalence of Diabetes, Impaired Fasting Glucose, and Impaired Glucose Tolerance in U.S. Adults: The Third National Health and Nutrition Examination Survey, 1988–1994." *Diabetes Care* 21 (1998).

Health Care Financing Administration. "Medicaid." Available from HCFA web site: http:www.hcfa.gov/medicaid/medicaid.htm.

Health Resources and Services Administration, Division of Disadvantaged Assistance, Centers of Excellence web site: http://www.hrsa.dhhs.gov/bhpr/dda/co efact.htm.

Hidalgo, M. "Language and Ethnicity in the 'Taboo' Region: the U.S.-Mexico Border." *International Journal of Sociology of Language* 114 (1995).

Hingson, R. et al. "Survey of AIDS Knowledge and Behavior Changes among Massachusetts Adults." *Preventive Medicine* 18 (1989), pp. 806–16.

Immigration and Naturalization Service. "Illegal Alien Resident Population." Available from INS web site: http://www.ins.usdoj.gov/graphics/a . . . s/statistics/illegal alien/index.htm"

Impact Consultants. *School-Based Survey Report for 6th and 10th Graders in Yuma County, Arizona, 1995.* Tucson, Ariz.: Impact Consultants.

Instituto Nacional de Estadística, Geografía, e Informática web site: www.inegi .gob.mx/economia/espanol/feconomia.html.

Ismail, A. I., and S. M. Szpunar. "The Prevalence of Total Tooth Loss, Dental Caries, and Periodontal Disease among Mexican Americans, Cuban Americans, and Puerto Ricans: Findings from HHANES 1982–1984." *American Journal of Public Health* 80, suppl. (1990).

Johnston, L. D., P. M. O'Malley, and J. G. Bachman. *The Monitoring the Future Study 1975–1998,* vol. 1. Washington, D.C.: U.S. Department of Health and Human Services, 1999.

Jórquez, J. S. "The Retirement Phase of a Heroin Using Career." *Journal of Drug Issues* 13 (1983), pp. 343–65.

Kass, B. L., R. M. Weinick, and A. C. Monheit. "Racial and Ethnic Differences in Health 1996." MEPS Chartbook No. 2. Available from Agency for Health Care Policy Research web site: www.meps.ahcpr.gov/papers/chartbk2/chartbk2a.htm.

Kegeles, S. M. et al. "Sexually Active Adolescents and Condoms: Changes over One Year in Knowledge, Attitudes, and Use." *American Journal of Public Health* 78 (1988), pp. 460–61.

Klor de Alva, J. J., "The Invention of Ethnic Origins and the Negotiation of Latino Identity, 1969–1981." In *Challenging Fronteras: Structuring Latina and Latino Lives in the United States,* eds. M. Romero, P. Hondagneu-Sotelo, and V. Ortiz, pp. 55–71. New York: Routledge, 1997.

Lecca, P. J., I. Quervalú, J. V. Nunes, and H. F. Gonzales. *Cultural Competency in Health, Social, and Human Services: Directions for the Twenty-First Century.* New York: Garland Publishing, 1998.

MacMillan, M. "Evaluation and Treatment of Patients from Nonwhite Ethnic Groups." Paper presented at the 132nd annual meeting of the American Psychiatric Association, Chicago, 1979.

Manoleas, P., ed. *The Cross-Cultural Practice of Clinical Case Management in Mental Health.* New York: Haworth Press, 1996.

Marin, G. "AIDS Prevention among Hispanics: Needs, Risk Behaviors, and Cultural Values." *Public Health Reports* 104 (1989), pp. 411–15.

——. "Defining Culturally Appropriate Community Interventions: Hispanics as a Case Study." *Journal of Community Psychology* 21 (1993), pp. 149–61.

Markides, K. S., D. J. Lee, and L. A. Ray. "Acculturation and Hypertension in Mexican Americans." *Ethnicity and Disease* 3, no. 1 (1993).

Martínez, O. J. *Border People: Life and Society in the U.S.-Mexico Borderlands.* Tucson: University of Arizona Press, 1994.

Mata, A. *Alcohol Use Among Rural South Texas Youth.* Austin, Tex.: Texas Commission on Alcohol and Drug Abuse, 1986.

Miranda, M. R., ed. *Psychotherapy with the Spanish-Speaking: Issues in Research and Service Delivery.* Spanish Speaking Mental Health Research Center Monograph No. 3. Los Angeles: University of California at Los Angeles, 1976.

Montoya, I. D., A. L. Estrada, A. Jones, and R. R. Robles. "An Analysis of Differential Factors Affecting Risk Behaviors among Out-of-Treatment Drug Users in Four Cities." *Drugs and Society* 9 (1996), pp. 155–71.

Moore, D. S., and P. I. Erickson. "Age, Gender, and Ethnic Differences in Sexual and Contraceptive Knowledge, Attitudes, and Behaviors." *Family and Community Health* 8 (1985), pp. 38–51.

Mosher, W. D., and J. W. McNally. "Contraceptive Use at First Premarital Intercourse: United States, 1965–1988." *Family Planning Perspectives* 23 (1991).

Myers, M. H. et al. "Report on Reliability of the AIDS Initial Assessment Questionnaire." In *Community-Based* AIDS Prevention. DHHS Pub. No. (ADM) 91-1752, pp. 167–82. Washington, D.C.: U.S. Department of Health and Human Services, 1991.

National Center for Health Statistics. *Deaths of Hispanic Origin: Vital and Health Statistics* ser. 20, no. 18 (1990).

——. *Health, United States, 1998 (with Socioeconomic Status and Health Chartbook).* Hyattsville, Md.: U.S. Department of Health and Human Services, 1998.

National Institute on Drug Abuse. *National Household Survey on Drug Abuse: Population Estimates 1991.* DHHS Pub. No. (ADM) 92-1887. Washington, D.C.: U.S. Department of Health and Human Services, 1991.

——. *Use of Selected Drugs among Hispanics: Mexican-Americans, Puerto Ricans, and Cuban Americans. Findings from the Hispanic Health and Nutrition Examination Survey.* Washington, D.C.: U.S. Department of Health and Human Services, 1987.

National Institutes of Health. *Drug Use among Racial/Ethnic Minorities.* NIH Pub. No. 98-3888. Bethesda, Md.: National Institutes of Health, 1998.

——. "Study First to Show Mexican Americans Hospitalized More Often for Heart Attack than Non-Hispanic Whites." NIH Pub. #97-4517. Bethesda, Md.: National Institutes of Health, 1997.

Negy, C., and D. J. Woods. "The Importance of Acculturation in Understanding Research with Hispanic Americans." *Hispanic Journal of Behavioral Sciences* 14, no. 2 (1992).

Nelson, C., and M. Tienda. "The Structuring of Hispanic Ethnicity: Historical and Contemporary Perspectives." In *Challenging Fronteras: Structuring Latina and Latino Lives in the United States,* eds. M. Romero, P. Hondagneu-Sotelo, and V. Ortiz, pp. 7–27. New York: Routledge, 1997.

Neufeld, D., Y.D.I. Chen, et al. "Early Presentation of Type 2 Diabetes in Mexican American Youth." *Diabetes Care* 21 (1998).

Novello, A. *Recommendations to the Surgeon General to Improve Hispanic/Latino Health.* Washington, D.C.: U.S. Department of Health and Human Services, Office of the Surgeon General, June 1993.

Orfield, G., and J. T. Yun. "Resegregation in American Schools." The Civil Rights Project, Harvard University. Available from Harvard University web site: www.law.harvard.edu/civilrights/publications/resegregation99.html.

Ortiz de Montellano, B. R. *Aztec Medicine, Health, and Nutrition.* New Brunswick, N.J.: Rutgers University Press, 1990.

Padilla, A. M., and V. N. Salgado de Snyder. "Hispanics: What the Culturally Informed Evaluator Needs to Know." In *Cultural Competence for Evaluators: A Guide for Alcohol and Other Drug Abuse Prevention Practitioners Working with Ethnic/Racial Communities,* eds. M. A. Orlandi, R. Weston, and L. G. Epstein, pp. 117–46. Rockville, Md.: U.S. Department of Health and Human Services, Public Health Service, Alcohol, Drug Abuse, and Mental Health Administration, 1992.

Padilla, E. R., and A. M. Padilla, eds. *Transcultural Psychiatry: An Hispanic Perspective.* Spanish Speaking Mental Health Research Center Monograph No. 4. Los Angeles: University of California at Los Angeles, 1977.

Park, J., and J. S. Buechner. "Race, Ethnicity, and Access to Health Care, Rhode Island," *Journal of Health and Social Policy* 9, no. 1 (1997).

Portes, A., and A. Stepick. "A Repeat Performance? The Nicaraguan Exodus." In *Challenging Fronteras: Structuring Latina and Latino Lives in the United States,* eds. M. Romero, P. Hondagneu-Sotelo, and V. Ortiz, pp. 135–51. New York: Routledge, 1997.

Pulido, L. *Environmentalism and Economic Justice: Two Chicano Struggles in the Southwest.* Tucson: University of Arizona Press, 1996.

Reichman, J. S. "Language-Specific Response Patterns and Subjective Assessment of Health: A Sociolinguistic Analysis." *Hispanic Journal of Behavioral Sciences* 19, no. 3 (August 1997).

Rodríguez, S. "The Hispano Homeland Debate Revisited." *Perspectives in Mexican American Studies* 3 (1992).

Rodríguez-Trias, H., and A. B. Ramírez de Arellano. "The Health of Children and Youth." Chap. 5 in *Latino Health in the United States: A Growing Challenge,* eds. C. W. Molina and M. Aguirre-Molina. Washington, D.C.: American Health Association, 1994.

Romero, M., P. Hodagneu-Sotelo, and V. Ortiz. *Challenging Fronteras.* New York & London: Routledge, 1997.

Schu, C. L., M. L. Burc, C. D. Good, and E. N. Gardner. *California's Undocumented Latino Immigrants: A Report on Access to Health Care Services.* Bethesda, Md.: The Project HOPE Center for Health Affairs, 1999.

Segura, D. A., and A. de la Torre. "La Sufrida: Contradictions of Acculturation and Gender in Latina Health." In *Revisioning Women, Health, and Healing,* eds. A. E. Clarke and V. L. Oleson. New York and London: Routledge, 1999.

Selik, R. M. et al. "Racial/Ethnic Differences in the Risk of AIDS in the United States." *American Journal of Public Health* 78 (1988), pp. 1539–45.

Singer, M. "Confronting the AIDS Epidemic among IV Drug Users: Does Ethnic Culture Matter?" *AIDS Education and Prevention* 3, no. 3 (1991), pp. 258–83.

———. "A Dose of Drugs, a Touch of Violence, a Case of AIDS: Conceptualizing the SAVA Syndemic." *Free Inquiry in Creative Sociology* 24, no. 2 (1996), pp. 99–110.

Singer, M. et al. "Culturally Appropriate AIDS Prevention of IV Drug Users and Their Sexual Partners." In *Community-Based AIDS Prevention.* DHHS Pub. No. (ADM)

91-1752, pp. 234–40. Washington, D.C.: U.S. Department of Health and Human Services, 1991.

Social Security Administration web site: http://www.ssa.gov/search97cgi, search keyword ssi.

Stevens, S. J., J. R. Erickson, and A. L. Estrada. "Characteristics of Female Sexual Partners of Injection Drug Users in Southern Arizona: Implications for Effective HIV Risk Reduction Interventions." *Drugs and Society* 7, no. 3/4 (1993), pp. 129–42.

Substance Abuse and Mental Health Services Administration (SAMHSA). *Data from the Drug Abuse Warning Network (DAWN).* 1994 Data File. Rockville, Md.: SAMHSA, 1994.

Sundquist, J., and M. A. Winkleby. "Cardiovascular Risk Factors in Mexican American Adults: A Transcultural Analysis of NHANES III, 1988–1994." *American Journal of Public Health* 89, no. 5 (1999).

Texas Department of Human Services web site: www.dhs.state.tx.us/programs/TexasWorks/pregnant.html.

Triandas, H. C. *The Analysis of Subjective Culture.* New York: John Wiley, 1972.

UPI. "Study: Risk of Coronary Disease Higher in Hispanics." UPI Science Report (November 8, 1998).

U.S. Bureau of the Census. *Current Population Survey, March 1997.* Washington, D.C.: Government Printing Office, 1997.

———. *Health Insurance Coverage: 1997,* Current Population Reports, Series P60-202. Washington, D.C.: Government Printing Office, September 1998.

———. *1990 Census of Population.* Washington, D.C.: Government Printing Office, 1990.

Vargas, R., and S. Martínez. *Razalogía: Community Learning for a New Society.* Oakland, Calif.: Razagente Associates, 1984.

Velasco, A. *Finding, Interviewing, and Retrieving Blood Samples from Tecatos: AIDS Prevention and Research in San Diego.* DHHS Pub. No. (ADM) 91-1752, pp. 121–25. Washington, D.C.: U.S. Department of Health and Human Services, 1991.

Weissman, G. et al. "Drug Use and Sexual Behaviors among Sex Partners of Injecting-Drug Users. United States, 1988–1990." *Mortality and Morbidity Weekly Report* 40, no. 49, (1991), pp. 855–60.

"What Is Medicare?" June 4, 1999. Available from Medicare web site: http://www.medicare.gov/whatis.html.

Williams, S. J., and P. R. Torrens, *Introduction for Health Services.* 2d. ed. New York: Wiley, 1984.

Youth Risk Behavior Survey. Atlanta, Ga.: CDC, 1995.

Zambrana, M. M. *Mejor Sola que Mal Acompañada: For the Latina in an Abusive Relationship.* Seattle: The Seal Press, 1985.

■ INDEX

Numbers in italics refer to illustrations.

wages, 88, 96n. 25
web of causation, 68
welfare reform, 82
wellness, 24
WHEEL (Women Helping to Empower and Enhance Lives), 65
witches, witchcraft, 24
women, 8, 37, 39, 41, 65; cultural identity and, 105–6; and domestic violence, 44–45; drug use by, 56, 57, 65; gender roles of, 106–8; health insurance and, xxix, 85–87, 121; health issues of, xxvi, 43, 48, 120; in medical schools, 91–92
working poor, xxviii, 83, 93, 121, 135
Wyoming, 7

youth, 61; drug abuse prevention and, 68–70; drug use and, xxvi, 58, 59, 64–65; socioeconomics and, 30–31. *See also* adolescents

ABOUT THE AUTHORS

ADELA DE LA TORRE, an agricultural economist, is director of the Mexican American Studies and Research Center at the University of Arizona. She is also a professor at the College of Public Health at the University of Arizona and directs the Border Academy, a summer institute that explores the unique characteristics of the U.S.-Mexico border. She received her Ph.D. in agricultural and resource economics in 1982 from the University of California, Berkeley. Her publications and research focus on health care access and finance issues that affect the Latino/a community. In 1999 she became the director of the Arizona Hispanic Center of Excellence in the College of Medicine at the University of Arizona. She is coeditor of the book *Building with Our Hands: New Directions in Chicana Scholarship,* published by the University of California Press in 1993.

ANTONIO ESTRADA is an associate professor of public health and Mexican American studies at the University of Arizona. Estrada received his master's and doctoral degrees in public health, graduating from the University of California, Los Angeles, in 1986. His primary interests are Hispanic health, focusing on health promotion and disease prevention within this population. He has written numerous publications and presentations on the subject of HIV/AIDS and Hispanics. Currently, Estrada is the principal investigator of a five-year study, funded by the National Institute on Drug Abuse (NIDA), to develop, implement, and assess a culturally innovative HIV/AIDS risk-reduction program targeting Mexican-origin Hispanic drug injectors and their female sexual partners in Tucson. He has also been chief investigator on several other NIDA-funded studies involving the National AIDS Demonstration Research Study, as well as an HIV/AIDS risk-reduction project on the U.S.–Mexico border.

Mexican Americans and Health is a volume in the series The Mexican American Experience, a cluster of modular texts designed to provide greater flexibility in undergraduate education. Each book deals with a single topic concerning the Mexican American population. Instructors can create a semester-length course from any combination of volumes, or may choose to use one or two volumes to complement other texts.

Additional volumes deal with the following subjects:

Mexican Americans and Economics
Arturo González

Mexican American History
Juan García

Chicano Popular Culture
Charles Tatum

Chicanos and the Environment
Devon Peña

Mexican American Identity
Aida Hurtado and Patricia Gurin

For more information, please visit
www.uapress.arizona.edu/textbooks/latino.htm